Session 1
The Growing Years

M000006195

Visitors at the Manger

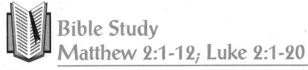

Bible Study
Matthew 2:1-12; Luke 2:1-20

If you were a newspaper or television reporter covering the story of Jesus' birth, you would need to get your facts straight. Reporters seek answers to the five W's:

Who? *(Who was there? Who saw it? Who did it?)*
What? *(What really happened? What did people think?)*
When? *(When did it happen? Year? Time? Day or night? Special season?)*
Where? *(Where did it occur? What was the reason it happened there? Was the place it happened important?)*
Why? *(What or who caused it to happen? Was there a reason or motive?)*

Turn to either Matthew 2:1-12 or Luke 2:1-20. Read the entire story. Then follow the instructions below:

WHO? As you read, check off from this list the names of the people who appear in the story in your passage.

__ Mary	__ Joseph
__ Innkeeper	__ Herod
__ Angels	__ Jesus
__ Wise men	__ Shepherds
__ Three kings	__ Harold the Angel

WHAT? Note carefully what happened. Don't include anything that isn't there. Put the events in their correct order.

First

Second

Next

Next

WHEN? According to your Scripture, when did this event take place? During what other significant event?

WHERE? Where exactly did this event occur? City, country, lodging, surroundings?

WHY? From clues you pick up from the story (not from anything you have learned elsewhere), tell why this event occurred where and when it did. What caused it, for example, to occur in Bethlehem? What was the reason for the event?

It's Good News!

You've done your research; now start your article. You may not have time to write it out in full, but you can get it started. Put in some key sentences that you would use in a full article.

You can also decide what style you might write it in. Here are some starters with headlines and the first lines of the articles. You take it from there.

The Science News Daily

BRIGHT STAR RUMORED OVER BETHLEHEM

Scientists report a bright star over the small city of Bethlehem; reports from people near the city indicate . . .

Rock 'n Roll News

MUSIC ROCKS SMALL TOWN SKIES

In what was rumored to be the greatest light and sound show ever, heavenly beings serenaded shepherds in a field near Bethlehem. The unexpected, unplugged performance played late into the night when the angels told the shepherds to . . .

The Star/Inquirer Gossip Weekly

ANGRY KING SEEKS NEWBORN RIVAL: RUMORS ABOUT DEATH PLOT

Waving his fist angrily in the air, King Herod commanded his troops to find a baby rumored to be born nearby. When asked why he was so upset about a child, the king babbled on about the child taking over his kingdom. The "story" as he told it is that . . .

SPORTS NEWS

GOD'S SNEAK PLAY SCORES WINNING RUN

In a play that would warm the hearts of any sports fan, the almighty God pulled a surprise sacrifice fly that turned out to be a game winner. Sliding secretly into the small town of Bethlehem, Mary and Joseph (two long-time members of the team) squeezed past Herod's defenses completely. In spite of careful training, Herod's team did not know how to cap off the victory, when it seemed to have the lead. Unknown to Herod, several fans were able to see the baby born to Joseph and Mary. To do this, they performed a trick play that went like this . . .

The Hotel Association News

BIG SURPRISE FOR
BETHLEHEM HOTEL OWNER

Simon Lazarus, chairman of the Bethlehem Tourist Association and local hotel owner, ought to be making big money soon. Lazarus reports that a young couple came to him for a room during the always hectic tax-paying season. Seeing a way to turn this into a little bit of business, Lazarus, whose hotel was already full, rented them space in his barn (how many of you would have thought of that?).

Well, it seems the woman was going to have a baby. But that's not the strangest part of it. Simon reports that that was the first of several unusual events that night. According to Lazarus, "Later in the night . . ."

Use the space below for your own report of what happened that night.

Session 2
The Growing Years

Visitors to the City

Bible Study
Luke 2:39-52

When Jesus was very young, his parents dedicated him at the Temple in Jerusalem according to their religious customs. Then they took him home to Nazareth. Verse 40 says that the child grew and became strong, that he was filled with wisdom, and that the favor of God was upon him. What do you think that means? Did Jesus not have a normal boyhood? Did he never get into trouble with his parents?

Verses 41-44 say that Jesus' parents were returning home from the annual trek to Jerusalem for Passover, when they discovered he wasn't with them. How would your parents react if you stayed some place without telling them? What can you guess about how people traveled in Jesus' day from the fact that his parents didn't miss him for an entire day?

When they discovered Jesus missing, his parents returned to Jerusalem. It took them three days to find him. What might they have been thinking and feeling while they were searching? When they found Jesus, he was in the Temple talking with teachers. How do you think his parents felt when they first saw him?

What did Jesus' parents say to him (verse 48)? What does that tell you about their frame of mind? What do you think your parents would have said to you?

Read Jesus' answer to his parents carefully (verse 49). What do you think he meant? Did he not want his parents to find him? Was he planning to remain at the Temple? Was he being sassy? What was he trying to tell his parents about himself?

Luke says (verse 52) that Jesus increased in wisdom and in years, and in divine and human favor. In your opinion, how does this story illustrate that?

Hear Ye, Hear Ye

Read the story, or parts of it, out loud. Read it first as though you were sympathetic with Jesus' parents and really thought that he had not behaved properly. Then read it from Jesus' viewpoint, and show that his parents missed the point. Show through tone of voice and gestures who deserved sympathy and who was in the wrong.

Jesus went back to Nazareth with his parents. What was his behavior like after this event (verse 51)? Do you think he gave in to his parents no matter what they asked of him?

Signs of Maturity

Here are three checklists. One asks you to identify the signs that show that a person is growing in wisdom; another, to tell what shows a person has found favor with other people. The last is for you to check the signs that a person has found favor with God. Don't spend a lot of time thinking each item over. Your first reactions will do.

SIGNS OF WISDOM

__ knows when to keep quiet

__ can be counted on by almost everybody

__ seems to plan well and have things done on time

__ exercises every day

__ eats plenty of vegetables

__ can tie own shoelaces

__ asks questions before jumping to conclusions

__ drinks only diet soft drinks

__ is able to learn from experience

__ is careful to whom he or she gives loyalty

SIGNS OF FAVOR WITH PEOPLE

__ is voted president of the class

__ is trusted by almost everybody

__ has a gang that always does what he/she says

__ gets a lot of babysitting jobs

__ has a lot of dates

__ dresses like everyone else, only better

__ has a new car that is always full of friends

__ is nearly every teacher's pet

__ gets chosen to represent the school at a meeting in Europe

__ has the best collection of CD's in the entire school

SIGNS OF FAVOR WITH GOD

__ prays daily

__ is loved and respected

__ becomes patient and wise

__ finds favor with people

__ never gets pimples or sunburn

__ is able to handle crises calmly

__ gets straight A's in school

__ is able to honestly care about others

__ seems unbothered by the opinions of others

Session 3
The Growing Years

At the River

Who Expects What of You?

Parents
Employers
Teachers
You
Friends
Boy or Girl Friend
Brothers and Sisters
Teammates (or Club Members)

Bible Study
Matthew 3:1-12

Everyone expects something from somebody. It's true now, and it was true in Jesus' time. God expected certain things from the Jewish people. John the Baptist told them what God expected.

Both leaders and common people came to the river to hear John preach. What some of them expected of God turned out to be wrong. John wanted the people to repent (verse 2). What does *repent* mean?

According to verse 5, who came to John and what did he do for them? Why?

Verses 7-10 tell about some other people who came. They were Pharisees (important people who made and enforced many religious rules) and Sadducees (wealthy priests and others who ruled the country). John told them to do three things. What do you think each means? (Circle one for each phrase.)

"Bear fruit." (*grow plums* or *do what's right*)

"Repent." (*look sad and glum* or *change your mind and behavior*)

"Don't presume to say to yourselves, 'We have Abraham as our ancestor.'" (*really Moses is your father* or *it isn't your nationality that shows you are God's people*)

Notice that John did not tell them to be baptized. Contrast baptism with bearing fruit, repenting, and not counting on the luck of where you were born. What's a key difference? Notice what the common people were doing when John baptized them (verse 6).

Which of these two sentences do you think best catches John's meaning?
   1. If you want to be God's people, your heart and your actions need to be right with God.
   2. If you want to be God's people, follow all the religious rules and rituals.

Bible Study
Matthew 3:13-17

Jesus came to the river while John was preaching. John had argued with the Pharisees and Sadducees. He told them that they did not really understand what God wanted. Now John discovers he needs to hear the same message himself.

In verse 11, John says that he baptizes people who need to repent. He also says someone else is coming who is mightier than he is. He expects someone to come who will baptize and who will act the way John thinks a truly great person should act. Surely, a truly great man won't need to be baptized himself.

In verse 13, Matthew tells about Jesus appearing. Read why he came. What does he want John to do?

Jesus does not do what John expects, even though John is a good man. What reason does Jesus give for asking John to baptize him?

What did John expect to have happen?

THOUGHT QUESTIONS

Do you think Jesus was baptized in order to get rid of his sins or because he planned to bear good fruit?

What do you think Jesus meant when he said he would be baptized in order to fulfill all righteousness (which means, to do what is right)? Why is baptism the right thing to do?

In what ways did John expect the wrong things?

After he was baptized, Jesus heard God's voice say to him, "This is my Son, the Beloved, with whom I am well pleased." Do you think God was pleased simply because Jesus had gone through with being baptized?

Bible Study
Matthew 4:1-11

You remember that when Jesus was baptized he heard the voice of God say, "This is my Son, the Beloved, with whom I am well pleased." After hearing something like that, you would expect everything that follows to go smoothly. But that was not the case.

Instead, Jesus had to figure out what it *meant* to be God's beloved son. As it turned out, it wasn't easy. Read on and follow the directions to find out more.

The First Temptation
Matthew 4:1-4

1. In this story, Jesus has just been baptized. God had called him "my Son, the Beloved." What happened next?

2. Jesus fasted for forty days and forty nights. What other events in the Bible lasted for forty days and forty nights?

3. Describe Jesus' condition when he was approached by the devil.

4. When you think about Jesus' condition, was there any good reason not to turn stones to bread? Would it have been wrong to eat?

5. How does hunger affect your ability to think, be friendly, or be faithful to your beliefs?

6. What do you think the devil would have thought if Jesus had done what he asked?

7. What do you think "One does not live by bread alone" means?

The Second Temptation
Matthew 4:5-7

8. In the second temptation Jesus is taken to the Temple, the most public place in Jerusalem. What does the devil tempt him to do there?

9. What do you think would happen if a crowd saw Jesus do what the devil tempted him to do? What would they have expected of Jesus from then on?

10. What emotions do you think Jesus felt when he was taken from the Temple only to face yet another temptation? What feelings do you have when people constantly put pressure on you to live up to their demands?

11. What do you think the devil was trying to tempt God to do at the Temple? What would it have proved if the devil could have gotten God and Jesus to do what he wanted?

The Third Temptation
Matthew 4:8-11

12. Describe the setting and events of the third temptation in your own words.

13. What did Satan offer to Jesus? What, in your opinion, did Satan really want?

14. Jesus turned down Satan's offer by saying that only God is to be worshiped. Why do you think worshiping God is more important than having power?

15. What happens when people seek power but do not worship God?

16. What do you think many of the leaders of our world today worship most of all?

17. As you consider your own life, what do you worship (that is, what seems to be most important to you)?

18. What do you know about Jesus from this story of the temptations?

Talent List

Here is a list of strengths and talents. Strengths and talents aren't always things at which you are better than anyone else. They are simply things you like to do and think you do well enough.

Circle the ones below that are *your* strong points. You may add to this list if you wish. Then put a star by the two that are most important to you.

friendship	car repair	debate
sports	computers	sewing
child care	video games	electronics
listening	chemistry	teaching
math	leadership	humor
poetry	cooking	reading
dancing	good follower	planning events
helpfulness	creating excitement	prayer
serving others	eating	counseling
music	weightlifting	woodworking
fashion	song writing	

Session 5
Calling the Disciples

At the Synagogue

"I Remember When . . ."

We all have had to deal with problems. Dig into your memory to recall problems you once had that would fit each of the four sentences below. Current issues are okay. You will have opportunity to talk about some of the things you write here.

1. One time when I really needed to hear some good news was . . .

2. One time when I really felt stuck and needed to find a way out was . . .

3. One time when I had a problem and just couldn't see any way out was . . .

4. One time when I felt people were coming down on me pretty hard was . . .

Bible Study
Luke 4:14-22

Give the answer you think is best, but don't spend too much time on any one—trust your first impressions. You will have to read along in the Bible in order to understand what the questions are asking.

1. At the beginning, Jesus went to Galilee. Galilee is
___ a small restaurant
___ a small woman named Lee
___ an area 60 miles north of Jerusalem
___ a city 60 miles north of Jerusalem

2. While in Galilee, Jesus went to a synagogue. A synagogue is
___ a place for synning
___ a place for sunning
___ a place of worship and learning
___ a place for training rabbis

3. Jesus went there on the Sabbath. The Sabbath is like our
___ Sunday
___ Wednesday night through Thursday
___ Friday night to Saturday evening
___ different times, depending upon when Easter falls

4. Jesus read out loud from the Book of Isaiah. Isaiah is
__ a book of proverbs (from the phrase "I say a")
__ a book of rules for Jewish worship
__ a famous prophet among the Jews
__ one of the first disciples

5. Jesus read that he was to preach good news to the poor. What, in your opinion, would be good news to people who are poor?

6. Jesus read that he was to proclaim release to the captives. Who do you think were the captives he was referring to?

7. Jesus said he was to bring sight to the blind. Do you think he meant that he was going to cure the eyes of people who cannot see? Why or why not?

8. How do you think Jesus intended to set free those who are oppressed?
__ Give everyone in prison freedom, no matter what the crime
__ Get religious people out of trouble
__ Help people and nations understand the needs of refugees, poor persons, and people who are unjustly in prison

9. When Jesus finished reading, he closed the book and said, "Today this Scripture has been fulfilled in your hearing." Which of these comes closest to stating what you think Jesus meant?
__ Starting immediately, all of the blind can see.
__ All of those statements have come true, but only the faithful can see how.
__ Starting at that moment, God was beginning to change the world to make these statements come true through Jesus.

10. When Jesus finished speaking, the people, who were all from his hometown, began to say nice things. But some said, "Is not this Joseph's son?" What do you think they meant?
__ I wondered who that was, but now I recognize him.
__ He's from our town, but look at the wonderful understanding he has.
__ He's just a local boy. Who does he think he is saying things like this?

11. Suppose you were asked by God to go to your own church (or even to this group), and tell them that there was to be freedom, healing, and help for the poor, and that God was going to start it all right then, through you. How would you feel?

12. How do you think the people in your church (or group) would respond?

13. Do you think we are supposed to do any of the things Jesus read about? Why or why not?

A Synagogue Worship Service

Today we will worship the way the Jews did in their synagogues. It was the way Jesus worshiped during his growing years, and it was also the way he worshiped on the day he stood to teach the people at Nazareth about himself.

1. Sing (or read) a psalm. Look in your hymn book for "The Lord's My Shepherd," Psalm 23.

2. Recite the Shema (Deuteronomy 6:4-5):

"Hear, O Israel: The LORD is our God, the LORD alone. You shall love the LORD your God with all your heart, and with all your soul, and with all your might."

3. From the Torah (the Law), read Exodus 20:8-11.

4. From the prophets, read Isaiah 58:6.

5. For the sermon, read Luke 4:16-21.

6. For the blessing, read Numbers 6:24-26 all together.

Calling the
Disciples

Starting a Movement

You are on the planning committee for a project that you hope is going to be very big—statewide, possibly even nationwide. You want to get it kicked off in a big way. Your committee members have given you a list of names of people they think would attract a good following. Which of these would you try to get first? Select at least ten.

Winona Ryder	Keanu Reaves
Garth Brooks	Mickey Mouse
Your plumber	The President of the US
Monica Seles	Jim Carrey
Oprah	Shaquille O'Neal
Your governor	Car mechanic
John Kennedy Jr.	Billy Graham
Amy Grant	Ken Griffey Jr.
Your pastor	Your mom
David Letterman	Jesse Jackson
A bishop	Mother Teresa
Hillary Rodham Clinton	Boyz II Men
Your principal	Denzel Washington

Name some others here if you like:

Be ready to give one reason for each of your choices.

Bible Study
Luke 5:1-11

Let's look at this story two ways. First, how did Jesus draw others to his movement? Second, who did Luke think would be attracted by that story to join the movement (the church)?

What Happened at the Lake?

1. What was Jesus doing at first?

2. Jesus got into a boat. Why?

3. Whose boat was it?

4. After teaching a while, Jesus told Simon Peter to put the nets in the water. What was his response?

5. If you were Simon Peter, what might you have thought when Jesus ordered you to put in your nets after an unsuccessful night's fishing?

6. Think about when you have been asked to do things that seemed utterly unrealistic. Were they like this situation? How did they turn out?

7. How did the fishing turn out for Peter? Who came to help?

8. If you'd had Peter's sudden good fortune, what would you have felt about Jesus? What was Peter's response? What do you think he was feeling?

9. Simon Peter and his partners, James and John, were astonished. Then Jesus told them something even more astonishing: "From now on you will be catching people." What do you think that means?

10. What was their response?

11. Do you think Jesus expected everyone to respond the way Peter, James, and John did? Why or why not?

12. In Jesus' time there were many wealthy and influential people—like the celebrities and stars of our time. There were big name religious leaders, important political figures, wealthy business owners, entertainers of many kinds. Fishermen, on the other hand, were usually poor, tough, unable to read or write, and had little influence. Why do you think Jesus started his movement by calling people like that to follow him?

What Happened With Luke?

Luke was not at all like the fishermen Jesus first called. Luke may have been a physician. He was wealthy and had wealthy friends. He was also well educated. Luke was one of the best writers in the New Testament.

Luke wrote his Gospel to help others understand Jesus. We know that there were many more stories about Jesus than Luke was able to tell. He had to choose which ones to include. That means he had to ask himself which stories would help people follow Jesus and join the church.

Jesus had risen quite a while before Luke began to write his Gospel. If you were Luke, and you were surrounded by many well educated, wealthy people, what would you want them to learn from the story in Luke 5:1-11? These questions will help you think about it.

1. With which sorts of people are we all most comfortable—those who are more like or more unlike ourselves? Would that be true of the church as well?

2. Peter may still have been alive when Luke wrote his Gospel. How do you think Luke's friends would react to having a fisherman be the leader of the church?

3. What might Luke have been telling his friends about true leadership in the church?

4. What might Luke have been wanting to tell his friends about the purpose of the church and about what they should be doing?

What's Happening With Us?

Jesus called the fishermen to a new job. They were to "cast their nets" not for fish but for people. Persons called by Jesus are to gather other people into the life of faith and the church.

Doesn't that make sense? When you experience something wonderful, you want others to do so also, right? If you find hope, help, and happiness in your faith in Christ and in your experience among other Christians, why not tell others? Why not gather them in?

Who do you know who is not now experiencing a life of faith within a church?

If the person is already a friend of yours, have you talked about faith with him or her? Have you offered an invitation to come to church or youth activities with you? If not, what is holding you back?

If the person is not a friend already, does he or she need a friend? Can *you* be a friend? Try this:

➤ Greet the person. (He or she may think you don't even know he or she exists!)

➤ Start conversations; find out more about your new friend.

➤ Include him or her in things you are doing.

➤ Pray for an appropriate opportunity to talk about faith and to invite this person to come with you to church or to other youth activities.

➤ Follow through: "Cast your net"—gather your new friend in.

Model of a
Disciple

Beatitude
(bee AH ti tood)

means something like
"to have good fortune"
and
"to be happy."
Some people talk about them as
"Beautiful Attitudes."

Who's Lucky?

1. Put a check by those you think are really lucky.
2. Select the five luckiest.
3. Then put them in order: 1 (the very luckiest) on down to 5.

__ the President

__ new parents

__ the homeless

__ nice people

__ good mechanics

__ handsome guys

__ beautiful girls

__ movie stars

__ people who make friends easily

__ people who never seem to be embarrassed

__ the richest family

__ people who can get away with anything

__ the poorest family

__ great musicians

__ "A" students

__ professional athletes

__ successful writers

__ kids with "cool" parents

__ high school athletes

__ kids with cars

__ people who know how to forgive others

__ people who tell the truth no matter what

__ kids with jobs

__ kids with happy homes

Who's Happy?

Complete these sentences with the first thoughts that come to your mind.

1. I think people are happy when

2. Three things that would make me happy are

3. I think the happiest people in the world must be those who

4. One thing I did that made someone else happy was

Bible Study
Matthew 5:1-12

Each beatitude spoken by Jesus has two parts:
➤ the name of those who will be blessed,
➤ the promise God makes to them.
The blessing they will get is that the promise will come true.

Here is a list of those who will be blessed and the blessing they are promised:

Poor in spirit/kingdom of heaven

Those who mourn/comfort

The meek/inherit the earth

Those who hunger for righteousness/be filled

Merciful/mercy

Pure in heart/see God

Peacemakers/be called children of God

Those persecuted for righteousness/kingdom of heaven

Those reviled, persecuted, and falsely accused/a great reward in heaven

Select one of the beatitudes and then follow these directions:

1. Write the phrase describing the group that will be blessed.

2. Tell what you think that phrase means. (Check the meaning of the key word or phrase in the "Word List" if you need to.)

3. Name some people or groups in today's world who are like those described in the beatitude.

4. What do you think they are being promised?

5. Imagine those people from question 3—where they live, what they do, what life is like for them.

6. Then describe in your own words what you think their lives would be like if this beatitude came true for them. How would their lives change? What would they say? What would they do?

7. If you were them, what would your feelings have been before and after the beatitude came true?

before:

after:

Word List

Poor in spirit. To be humble.

Kingdom of heaven. The presence of God and the place where things are as God wants them.

Those who mourn. Those who are deeply unhappy, usually because of a loss.

The meek. Those who are not greedy and do not demand more of the world than they need.

Righteousness. Following God's will, especially being fair and doing justice.

Pure in heart. Dedicated to God. Faithful and honest.

To see God. To experience God.

In heaven. To be with God.

Children of God. Those who are admitted into fellowship with God.

WILL WORK FOR FOOD

The Secret of Worship

Worship Questionnaire

Worship services often include several of the elements below. Rate how meaningful and interesting you find each.

1 = Booorrriiinnnggg! (not interesting or meaningful at all.)

2 = Ho hum. (interesting or meaningful once in a while)

3 = So-so. (interesting or meaningful half of the time)

4 = Cool! (usually interesting or meaningful)

5 = Nothing on earth could make me stop! (always interesting and meaningful)

1. Music	1 2 3 4 5
2. Singing	1 2 3 4 5
3. Confession and Words of Assurance	1 2 3 4 5
4. Joys and concerns	1 2 3 4 5
5. Silent prayer	1 2 3 4 5
6. The Lord's Prayer	1 2 3 4 5
7. Announcements	1 2 3 4 5
8. Children's time	1 2 3 4 5
9. Scripture readings	1 2 3 4 5
10. Pastor's prayers	1 2 3 4 5
11. Offering	1 2 3 4 5
12. Sermon	1 2 3 4 5

1. What do you think *worship* means?

2. To truly worship, how much depends upon what is happening in the service and how much depends upon what is happening inside you?

3. What would help you be able to worship more fully in the Sunday morning worship service?

"And the Churchie Award for Best Worshiper Goes to . . ."

St. Pumpkins by the Vine Church has decided to give an award to the truest worshiper in the congregation. They have narrowed it down to three finalists. Because you don't go to St. Pumpkins and therefore won't show any favoritism, they have asked you to be on the panel of judges. To whom would you give the award?

MOLLY MICKLER. Molly never misses a worship service, even when she is ill. People marvel at her faithfulness. She is also very generous to the church and is often the first to announce her gift during the annual fund drive. She prays earnestly and quietly for the church. Last year, during Lent she gave up eating lunches and was an inspiration to all.

FRED FREEBONES. Fred has given generously to help many families in the community—although only the pastor knows (one of the families told him). One year he gave up his vacation in order to give the money to the youth mission trip fund. Fred is also great at praying. People talk about how wonderful his prayers are whenever he helps lead worship. Fred usually practices his prayers before a mirror so he will get every tone and gesture right. He chooses words that will, as he says, "really wow them."

PERRY PERFECT. Perry has a gentle spirit. He prays often. His heart goes out to the ill, the weak, and those with problems; and he includes them on his prayer list every morning and evening. He also has learned that possessions can become too important. So, each Lent he tries to find out what he has that gets in the way of his loyalty to God, and he gives that up—which he does privately, because it is just between God and him. Perry does not give very much money to the church or to charity. He does not believe in pledging. But whenever the pastor announces in worship that there is a needy family or that the church needs a new roof, Perry is the first to march up the aisle and put a check in the offering basket.

Bible Study
Matthew 6:1-18

God   or   Others

In the Scriptures Jesus tells us something about true and false worship. In true worship, we are the actors and we know that God is the audience. In false worship, we are the actors and we act as though other people are the audience. When God is the audience, we try to please God. When others are the audience, we try to please them.

Matthew 6:2-4 has to do with giving gifts for the poor. When the hypocrites give their gifts, they act as though their audience is

God   or   Others

Who should be their audience?

What do you think this phrase means: "But when you give alms, do not let your left hand know what your right hand is doing, so that your alms may be done in secret"?
__ During the offering, keep one hand in your pocket.
__ Only talk to one hand at a time.
__ Don't make a big deal out of helping someone.
__ Never let anyone know what you give.

Matthew 6:5-6 talks about prayer. Who is the audience for the prayers of the hypocrites?

God   or   Others

Who should the audience be?

What do you think Jesus meant when he said, "But whenever you pray, go into your room and shut the door and pray to your Father who is in secret"?
__ You can only pray in your room.
__ People without their own rooms cannot pray.
__ Don't show off when you pray.
__ Never let anyone see you pray.

Matthew 6:16-18 deals with fasting (which is not the opposite of slowing). Who is the audience for hypocrites when they fast?

God   or   Others

Who should their audience be?

When Jesus said, "But when you fast, put oil on your head and wash your face, so that your fasting may be seen not by others but by your Father who is in secret," what did he mean?

__ Oiling your hair and washing your face pleases God.
__ When you diet, don't tell anyone.
__ When you give up things to please God, don't go around bragging about it.
__ Never let anyone know when you give up something in order to please God.

Word List

Alms. Money, food gifts given to poor people.
Dismal. Gloomy, miserable.
Fast. To eat very little or nothing.
Gentiles. People who are not Jews.
Hypocrites. People who pretend to be what they are not.
Piety. Religious devotion and reverence for God.
Synagogue. A Jewish place of worship and learning.

Finding the Kingdom

Lost and Found

Everyone loses something sometime.

Everyone finds something sometime.

And once in a while, we find something that we have lost. When we do, it's usually something we have missed, looked for, gotten mad about, asked others to help us find, and needed right away. In fact, it seems like those are the things we lose the most!

Recall something you lost and then found. It may be big or small in size, but it must be something that was important, something that mattered to you. The questions below will help jog your memory. Jot some notes if you need to; then be ready to tell the story of your experience.

Why was the object so important to you?

When and how did you discover it was lost?

How did you feel when you first knew it was lost?

What steps did you take to find it? To whom did you talk?

Where did you begin to look?

What went through your mind as you searched?

What worries did you have?

How was the object found? by whom?

How did you feel when it was found?

What did you do when it was found?
- __ shouted
- __ hugged the finder
- __ said a prayer
- __ jumped around
- __ called a friend
- __ hugged myself
- __ told my parents
- __ other:

Bible Study
Matthew 13:44-46

Here are two very short stories about the king-dom of heaven. Neither Jesus nor Matthew, the Gospel writer, filled in the details. So you get to!

Work with either Matthew 13:44 or Matthew 13:45-46. Your job is to make a full story out of your verses—a story that you can tell the rest of the group. Use your imagination. The questions below are just starters.

The Case of the Hidden Treasure
Matthew 13:44

What was the man doing that led up to his find-ing the treasure? (What was he doing on some-one else's land? Was he taking a short cut? Was he a servant or a field hand?)

How did he happen to find the treasure? (Was he digging around? Did he just stumble across it?) And what was the treasure?

How did he feel when he found it?

When he found the treasure, who did he tell? Who didn't he tell? Who was he tempted to tell?

How did he sell all that he had? A yard sale? An auction? Did he sell it piece by piece? How did he make certain he got enough money?

During the time between finding the treasure and buying the land, he had to get a lot done. It took some time. What do you suppose kept him going?

Who did he tell about his treasure after he bought the field? How did he tell them? How did he celebrate, if he did?

The Case of the Purchased Pearl
Matthew 13:45-46

Where was the merchant searching for pearls? Was he a deep sea diver? (Did he buy oysters at the supermarket and open them? Was he at a gathering of rich and famous people auctioning off their jewelry?)

Did he find the pearl by accident? Had he heard a rumor that a great pearl might be found at this place?

How could he tell when he had a pearl of great value? What does that tell you about this man? Was he experienced at handling wealth? Did he just happen to be a reader of books about oysters?

How did he feel when he found the one great pearl?

How did he arrange to sell what he owned? (Rummage sale?) What kinds of things do you suppose he owned? (Jewelry? Used comic book collection?)

Who did he tell about his big find? (No one? A few close friends and business partners?) Who was he tempted to tell? Who would he never tell?

Who did he tell after he made the purchase? How did he tell them? How did he celebrate, if he did?

Amazing Grace

Amazing grace! How sweet the sound
That saved a wretch like me!
I once was lost, but now am found;
Was blind, but now I see.

Through many dangers, toils, and snares,
I have already come;
'Tis grace hath brought me safe thus far,
And grace will lead me home.

Lyrics by John Newton, 1779.

The Loving Father

Meet the Cast of Characters

Tax collectors. They were among the most hated of all people in Jewish society. Tax collectors got their positions by bidding for them. The one who paid the most to the ruler got the job. Tax collectors usually became very rich by tricking people and keeping part of the taxes they collected. The Jews considered tax collectors unclean and would not allow them even to give to charity, to be witnesses at a trial, or to sit and eat with other Jews.

Sinners. People were judged sinners if they did not obey the Law (Torah) and the many other religious rules followed by all faithful Jews. Sinners had to go through special religious services in order to be forgiven and cleansed. Otherwise, good Jews could not associate with them.

Pharisees. These men were devoted to living their religion as faithfully as possible. The Pharisees carefully followed the Law and the rules of the Jewish religion, gave generously of their possessions, and tried to remain pure. They were laymen, often having small businesses. The common people respected them highly.

Scribes. Highly honored and well-educated teachers of the Jewish law, scribes gave advice about the law. Students underwent a long education, and had to demonstrate much knowledge before they could be accepted as scribes. The common people respected the scribes so highly that they often stood in the streets as scribes passed by. Scribes had seats of honor in the synagogues.

The father. The father was a wealthy landowner and farmer. He had many servants. He followed the law and willingly divided his land between his sons as the law said.

The younger son. He grew restless with farm life and wanted out. Jewish law gave him the right to have one-third of his father's possessions as an inheritance.

The older son. Jewish law gave the oldest son two-thirds of his father's wealth. Along with that came the responsibility of caring for the remaining family.

Bible Study
Luke 15:1-2, 11-32

View From the Outer Circle

You are scribes and Pharisees. Now, imagine yourselves on the day Jesus told the story of the loving father.

Even though you know Jesus has gotten quite close to the tax collectors and sinners, you've heard about his reputation as a good teacher. You respect wisdom, and you're curious.

As Jesus tells the story, you begin to suspect that something is wrong. At least, something doesn't fit with the way you have been taught. Who, in the story, does Jesus seem to say the tax collectors and sinners are like?

According to your beliefs as scribes and Pharisees, what should happen to the younger son?

According to your beliefs as scribes and Pharisees, what should the father do when the boy returns home?

If the father is a symbol for God, how do you think God treats tax collectors and sinners?

What is your opinion of Jesus when you hear him telling everyone that the father (God) accepted his son (tax collectors and sinners) back with joy, even before the son had a chance to ask forgiveness for his sin?

When Jesus tells the second part of his story, you discover that Jesus thinks *you* are like the older son. Do you think the father treated the older son fairly or unfairly? Why?

If the older son stands for you, do you think you are being treated fairly?

As Jesus finishes the story, you become more aware of the sinners and tax collectors in the inner circle around Jesus. What do you think Jesus is telling you about your relationship with them?

What do you think he is telling them about their relationship with you?

What he is telling you both about God's relationship with you?

View From the Inner Circle

You have not been a very religious person during your life. But you were brought up by religious parents, and you have often felt a little guilty about not keeping up with the religious laws.

On the other hand, being a tax collector has paid off pretty well. The people don't like you, but, hey, you can buy nearly everything you want.

You have found a strange thing today, however. A rabbi (Jewish teacher) has started talking to you (that's strange, because no religious person is supposed to have anything to do with you). He has begun telling a story.

At first, it seems like another story in which there are bad guys and good guys—and it's easy to tell that the bad guy in the story (the younger son) is supposed to represent you.

Knowing you are not liked by religious people and that the younger son in the story stands for you, what do you expect to happen to the younger son?

The younger son ends up feeding pigs (pigs are considered unclean by the Jews); do you think that shows how the scribes and Pharisees think of you? Why or why not?

When Jesus starts to tell about the younger son going home, what do you expect to have happen when he gets there?

When the younger son arrives home, how does he feel about the way his father greets him?

If the younger son represents you, does this match with the way you think God will greet you? Why or why not?

When Jesus starts to tell about the older son, you become aware of the scribes and Pharisees standing around you. What do you think Jesus is telling you about your relationship with them?

What is he telling them about their relationship with you?

What is he telling you both about God's relationship with you?

Meet the Cast of Characters

The lawyer. This man was not like a present-day lawyer—a specialist in the laws of the land. He was a specialist in the Law of Moses. He was probably also a Pharisee, for the Pharisees took the Law very seriously. They studied it and they also preserved many of the important teachings about it. When a lawyer like this asked, "Who is my neighbor?" he wanted to know if the person who answered his question really knew the Law and the teachings of the Jewish people.

The priest. The priests served in the Temple in Jerusalem. According to Jewish law, a priest who touched a dead person made himself unclean. He could not serve as a priest until he had gone through a long period of cleansing. Therefore, if there were any doubt about whether a person were alive or dead, the priests dared not risk touching the body. This priest may have been on his way to take his turn serving at the Temple, and he could not have served if he were unclean.

The Levite. He was a member of the tribe of Levi, who also served in the Temple. Levites were not priests, but they could do some of the lesser services and duties. Their income often came from the tithes (offerings) they were given for their work in the Temple. Like the priests, they could not serve in the Temple if they were unclean. So the Levite too dared not risk touching a person who might possibly be dead.

The Samaritan. Originally Jews, people who lived in Samaria continued to use the first five books of the Bible (Torah) as the basis of their religion. Foreigners settled in their land and, after a while, began to marry and have families with the Samaritans. From that time on, Jews regarded them as impure. There was great hatred between Jews and Samaritans. Samaritans refused to worship at the Temple in Jerusalem and would not even give water to a Jewish pilgrim walking through Samaria on the way to the Temple. The Jews, for their part, were equally harsh. The word *Samaritan* was used as a swear word by Jews.

 **Bible Study**
Luke 10:25-37

Meet the Lawyer
Luke 10:25-26

Be the young lawyer who has approached Jesus. What made you decide to go to Jesus to ask your question?
__ Just curiosity
__ A sincere desire to know what the Law teaches about "Who is my neighbor?"
__ A plan to trick Jesus and show that he doesn't really know the Law
__ Like any good lawyer, I enjoy careful argument with a good opponent.

Why did you call Jesus "Teacher"?
__ It was flattery, to get him off guard.
__ Jesus is called "rabbi," which means "teacher."
__ I knew he did not have as good an education as I had, and calling him "Teacher" was a put-down.

___ I wished to show respect for his wisdom; after all, he had a wonderful reputation for wisdom and clear thinking.

The answer Jesus gave you was one that you had heard all of your life. He told you to love God and to love your neighbor. But you went on to ask him, "Who is my neighbor?" Why did you do that?

___ His answer was so common anyone could have said it. I wanted to find out if Jesus had any original thoughts.

___ In any area with so many kinds of people, it isn't always easy to tell who your neighbor is and who your enemy is; I wanted to learn how to tell.

___ We have many enemies who never treat us kindly. I truly need to know how I can tell who to trust as my neighbor.

___ There is clear teaching in our law. Only Jews are our neighbors. I wanted to see if he knew that.

Walk in Their Shoes
Luke 10:30-35

There is an old saying: You don't understand other people until you've walked in their shoes for a while. What would it be like to be one of the characters in Jesus' story of the good Samaritan? Finding that out could help you understand the parable, and it would also help make clear what its message is to us. Follow these steps:

1. Be the wounded man. Retell the story in first person. These questions will help you. Where were you going? What happened to you? What did you think after you were hurt? What went through your mind as you saw a priest from your own Temple coming down the road? What did you think when he passed you by? How about the Levite? What did you expect when you looked again and saw a Samaritan coming? What did you think when he came to your aid? Did you want him to touch you? How did your mind change about Samaritans?

2. Be the priest. These questions will help you retell the story from his point of view. Where were you going? What had you been doing? When did you first notice the man lying by the side of the road? What went through your mind when you saw him there? Did you think of the commandment to love your neighbor? What prevented you from helping your fellow Jew at this time? How did you feel, having to pass by the side of the road and leave him there?

3. Be the Levite. What do you do for a living? Where were you when you saw the wounded man? What went through your mind when you saw him? You know that you should love your neighbor; what prevented you from helping this man? How did you feel, having to leave him by the side of the road in order to protect your own living?

4. Be the Samaritan. You are on the road to Jericho. You see a wounded man. What is your first thought? When you look closer you see he is a Jew; what do you think then? You can't tell whether he is alive or dead; why do you reach out to him? How do you feel, knowing that you have touched a person who is unclean to you (he is a Jew) and that you are now unclean as well? In your mind you know two commandments of the Law—one to love your neighbor and another to remain pure. You had to choose between the two. Why did you choose the one you did?

Back to the Lawyer
Luke 10:36-37

You have asked Jesus your question, and he has told you the story of the good Samaritan as his answer. Jesus asks you a question now: Which of these three proved a neighbor to the man who fell among robbers? What is your answer?

How do you feel when Jesus uses a Samaritan to show you how to follow the law and be a neighbor?

__ Just wonderful. I always wanted to know who my neighbor is, and now I know.

__ Terrible. How dare he hold up a lousy Samaritan as an example to me?

__ Excited. I have a brand new insight into what neighborliness means.

__ Frightened. I don't think I have what it takes to be that kind of neighbor.

Jesus then tells you to go and do likewise. Do you do it? Why or why not?

Nicodemus

Bible Study
John 3:1-15

Jesus is talking with Nicodemus, a leader of the Jews. What does Nicodemus ask Jesus? What does Jesus ask Nicodemus? Write the questions and the answers below. Some of the questions are not answered directly in the Scripture. What do you think would be the answers given?

JESUS

Questions   Answers

NICODEMUS

Questions   Answers

What do you think these two sayings of Jesus mean?

1. "What is born of the flesh is flesh, and what is born of the Spirit is spirit" (verse 6).

2. "The wind blows where it chooses, and you hear the sound of it, but you do not know where it comes from or where it goes. So it is with everyone who is born of the Spirit" (verse 8).

Verses 14-15 refer to an episode in the Old Testament (Numbers 21:4-9). The Israelites had sinned greatly and were punished by deadly snake bites. When the people cried out, sorry for their sin, God told Moses to make a serpent out of bronze and lift it high on a pole. Whenever a snake bit someone, that person would look in faith at the bronze serpent and live. God had provided a means of forgiveness and healing. It required only the faith of people.

3. What do you think Jesus means in verses 14-15 when he says, "And just as Moses lifted up the serpent in the wilderness, so must the Son of Man be lifted up, that whoever believes in him may have eternal life"?

46

What Do You Think He Meant?

Read the Bible verses listed below. Write a letter "A" if you agree that the sentence explains the verse correctly, and a letter "D" if you disagree with the sentence. You may find yourself agreeing with more than one sentence.

Verse 2 says that Nicodemus came at night time. This means
__ he just got off from work;
__ he didn't want anyone to see him;
__ John used darkness to symbolize Nicodemus' ignorance;
__ it probably means nothing at all.

Read what Nicodemus says to Jesus in verse 2. When he says that, Nicodemus is trying to
__ get into Jesus' confidence;
__ prepare a trap;
__ let Jesus know that he has been watching him for a while;
__ show respect for Jesus, whom he regards as a teacher like himself.

Read verse 3. Jesus tells Nicodemus that he must be born from above. The phrase "from above" could also be translated
__ again
__ anew
__ afresh
__ miraculously

In verse 5 when Jesus talks about being born of water and the Spirit, he means
__ you have to be baptized;

__ you don't have to be baptized, the Spirit will take care of everything;
__ baptism by water is important, but God's Spirit must also be in your life;
__ the kingdom of God is only for spirits.

Read verses 9-10. You can tell from the way Jesus answers Nicodemus that he intends to
__ insult him
__ tease him
__ inform him
__ keep a good conversation going

In verse 11 Jesus uses the word *we*. To whom is he referring?
__ Nicodemus and himself
__ all truly religious people
__ the disciples and Jesus

Read verse 12. Jesus refers to earthly and heavenly things. By those words he means
__ water and Spirit;
__ easy things to believe and harder things to believe;
__ truths about earthly life and about the kingdom of God;
__ himself and Nicodemus.

In verse 13, Jesus means
__ that he is the Son of Man;
__ that he started out in heaven and will end up there;
__ no one but Jesus will go to heaven;
__ no one is better able to help others experience heaven.

The meaning of this entire passage can be summed up this way:

__ Nicodemus and Jesus had a good debate, but nothing was settled.

__ Intelligent Jews appreciated Jesus, but they didn't always understand him.

__ Jesus respected the wise teachers of the Jewish faith, but knew that his ideas went beyond theirs.

__ Jesus brought the chance for a fresh beginning to people, and it would come to people if they believed in him, even if they didn't understand it.

You: Before and After

You've seen those commercials that show before and after. Someone's going bald. Then there is the same person with a full head of hair. Or someone looks really pitiful and then after the great makeover is completely different—and of course smiling!

You probably don't need more hair or a makeover. But aren't there some "befores and afters" you would like in your life? What would you like to change about yourself? Remember, when Jesus said, "You must be born again" he was telling us all that we can start over, start fresh, start out anew with help from above.

In the box labeled "Before" draw a symbol of some part of your life you'd like to get behind you—a habit, an embarrassing experience that keeps cropping up, an argument with a friend, something you perceive as a failing (for example, an alarm clock jangling to show a habit of being late, or a school paper with a bad grade).

In the box entitled "After" draw a symbol of what you might do or how you would feel if you could get a fresh start and do it right this time. You might show the alarm clock set earlier, or the paper with a gold star on it.

BEFORE

AFTER

Men and Women

In Jesus' Time

Put a check by the statements below that you think are true.

In Jesus' time:

1. __ Women in religious families of Jerusalem stayed in the house almost all of the time.

2. __ In Jerusalem, a groom didn't see his bride with her head uncovered until the day of their wedding.

3. __ The royal families were the least religious, and royal women had the greatest freedom.

4. __ Even young women from very religious families could go to two dances each year.

5. __ Sometimes husbands and wives could work together at a trade.

6. __ Husbands and wives could work together in the fields, but wives could not talk with passers-by.

7. __ The wealth of the father passed only to the sons.

8. __ Women often married before they were twelve years old.

9. __ Girls under twelve and a half had to marry whomever their fathers chose for them.

10. __ Cousins were able to marry one another.

11. __ Girls over twelve and a half could not be forced to marry.

12. __ In Jerusalem, fathers could sell their daughters under twelve into slavery.

13. __ Men often had to pay a woman's father for the right to marry her.

14. __ Men and women, once engaged, were treated like husband and wife.

15. __ In general, women were viewed as the property of men.

16. __ A married couple lived with the groom's family.

17. __ A husband owned whatever his wife earned or received as a gift.

18. __ A husband could force his wife to make a vow.

19. __ If a husband forced his wife to make a vow that violated her reputation or that of her family, she could divorce him.

20. __ In case of danger to the family, the husband must be saved first.

21. __ If a husband was not satisfied with his wife and also did not want a divorce, he could take a second wife into his home.

22. __ Marriage contracts included clauses telling how much the husband had to give the wife if he divorced her.

23. __ When marriages broke up, the children usually went with their father.

24. __ When a woman became a widow, she had to either marry her husband's brother or else get permission from the brother to marry someone else.

25. __ Women generally did not study the Torah (the first five books of the Bible, which the Jews regarded as the most holy of books).

26. __ Schools were only for boys.

27. __ Women were permitted to enter the synagogue.

28. __ Some girls were allowed to study Greek.

29. __ For forty days after they gave birth to a boy and eighty days after they gave birth to a girl, women could not enter the Temple in Jerusalem.

30. __ Only men could teach in the synagogues.

31. __ When a Jewish woman left her home in Jerusalem, she was expected to wear two veils, a head band, and a hair net to keep her features completely hidden.

32. __ Rabbis were not expected to have women as students or women in their groups.

33. __ In their homes unmarried women were confined to the innermost areas; their mothers could go into the outer rooms.

34. __ In general, rural people were not so strict about the roles of men and women as city people were.

35. __ Generally, unmarried men were not alone with women outside their own families.

Bible Study

Read the three Bible stories below. As you do, keep track of anything in them that breaks the rules for men and women listed in "In Jesus' Time."

Luke 10:38-42

If you were a follower of Jesus back then, what might you have learned from seeing this?

Mark 7:24-30

If you were a follower of Jesus then, what might you have learned from seeing this?

Mark 14:3-9

If you were a follower of Jesus' then, what might you have learned from seeing this?

In these stories, Jesus has treated the relationship between women and men in a new way. In your own words, tell what that new way is. How would it improve life for both men and women?

As a follower of Jesus today, what do these stories say to you?

If our society were to follow Jesus, what changes would there be in how women today would be treated?

Something Extra

Check out John 4:1-42. Jesus was constantly turning social rules upside down. Even the disciples who were closest to him were surprised. Look at verse 27!

The Wealthy

Lifestyles of the Famous and Wealthy

Most of us aren't wealthy—although some of us are. But all of us have some idea about wealthy people—really wealthy people. Think of those sleek, slim, and well-to-do people on TV shows, in the movies, or in magazines. Think about fast cars, jet planes, servants, polo ponies, and all the high-tech gadgets anyone could want.

Think about yourself with all that glitter and glitz. Let your mind go, and then complete the sentences below.

When I think about having all of that money, it makes me feel

The first five things I'd buy are

If I had all of that money, my clothes would all be

When it comes to transportation, you'd never see me in anything less than a

I think I would hire someone to

Frankly, for a person with a lot of money, I think the most important thing is

Of course, if I became really rich, some of my friends would

One thing I would worry about if I were rich is

Something I have always wondered about with those rich people in movies and on television is

Sometimes, when I see the lifestyles of rock stars and others, it makes me think

Still, all things considered, it is better by far to be wealthy than not to be wealthy (yes/no).

Suds Song (A Little Soap Opera)

Here are some starters for episodes of a soap opera. You tell what happens next.

Channel 1

Mary: John, isn't life wonderful? Yesterday we were poor, and today, thanks to your uncle's will, we have everything we'll ever need. (*Pause*) John? Why aren't you happy? Is something wrong?

John: It isn't that simple. I've been trying to tell you, but, well, you've been so happy I haven't had the heart. You see, the will *did* leave me the money . . .to care for, *not* to spend. In fact, it all has to be spent for the new hospital, every penny of it. And I have to be the one to do it. I spent all afternoon figuring it out. It's going to take every penny we have. You see, I have to be responsible for watching over the spending, and it's such a big job, I have to quit the company to find the time to do it. Mary, it's going to cost us every cent we have to do what that will says.

Mary: But John . . . (*You take it from here.*)

Channel 2
Nancy: (*shouting*): Frank! Frank! For heaven's sake, get off the yacht for a minute and come and take a look.

Frank: (*wearily*): Yeah, yeah. What's up? Can't you see I need a little sleep? I've been busy doing the bookkeeping for all of the condominium units we own. That's a tough job. And you know how those folks hate to pay their fees. I've nearly had to threaten some of them. Now, just when I get a minute off, you come in here screaming.

Nancy: All right, but you're going to miss it. Mother Teresa is coming by here and. . . . My heavens, she's coming my way. I think I should run away. No, I want to see her. I'll hide behind this large shed they're repairing. (*Pause*) Oh, no! She's stopping here. She's looking right at me. FRANK! She wants to come to our yacht for dinner.

Frank: But! . . . (*You finish the rest.*)

Bible Study
Luke 19:1-10

Jesus and the Wealthy Tax Collector

Check all that are true about Zacchaeus:
__ He was rich.
__ He was an upright business man.
__ He was excited to see Jesus.
__ He could stand on his tip-toes and see Jesus over the heads of the crowd.

Zacchaeus planned on seeing Jesus. Do you think he expected Jesus to see him? Why or why not?

If you had been Zacchaeus, what would have been your first reaction when Jesus saw you and told you to come down? The people who saw what happened grumbled. What did they say, and what did it mean?

In the presence of Jesus, Zacchaeus pledged to make a change in his life and business dealings. What did he say he would do?

> **Tax Collector.** Tax collectors were Jews who worked for the Romans, who ruled over Israel. Most took more money than required from the people, so they became rich while the people became poorer. The people hated them.

Jesus said, "Today salvation has come to this house." Which of these comes closest to what you think Jesus meant?

__ I, Jesus, have come to visit your home.

__ God's grace is there for you; you show you have accepted it in your willingness to change and make up for your cheating in the past.

__ You have learned to possess wealth without being possessed by it; you have shown that you understand what God wants.

Jesus indicated that Zacchaeus has been among the "lost." What do you think Jesus meant by that?

Jesus and the Rich Young Man
Mark 10:17-25

Here's another story where Jesus deals out some surprises!

From what you read in verse 17, what would you say was the young man's attitude toward Jesus? What evidence do you have?

Do you think the young man's question was sincere (yes/no)? Why?

Read the answer Jesus gave the young man in verse 19. Does that mean, in your opinion, that following the commandments is what God requires of all who wish to have eternal life?

The young man had kept the commandments. How did Jesus feel about him when he found that out?

Read all of verses 21-22. What did Jesus tell the young man?

Why do you think Jesus told him what he did?

The young man went away unhappy. Why?

Read verses 23-25. What do you think Jesus is saying about wealth?

Why do you think this would have surprised the disciples?

THOUGHT QUESTION

Jesus met two wealthy men. One he told to sell what he had, give it to the poor, and come and follow him. The other he allowed to keep his wealth (although the man chose to give half of his wealth to the poor) did not ask him to become a disciple, and announced that salvation had come to him. What, in your opinion, is the reason these two rich men were treated differently?

GET WELL SOON!

The Ill

Health Check

Think back to a time when you were ill. Not just a cold, but something that kept you home from school. Maybe you were even in the hospital for a while. It may have been a bug, an accident, or something really major. Do your best to remember, and then answer the following questions:

How long were you ill?

How did you feel emotionally when you first became ill?

How did you feel during the worst of it?

How did you feel when you began to improve?

How did you feel once it was all over?

Usually when persons are sick, they have several different kinds of needs. Who was the most important person in meeting each of these needs for you when you were ill?

Physical needs _____

Homework/other school needs _____

Tender loving care needs _____

Bright thoughts/encouragement _____

Letters/notes/phone calls _____

Transportation _____

How did you pass the time of day during your illness?

How did your religious beliefs affect you during your illness? Check all that apply:
__ Did you pray? __ Think about God? __ Wonder why folks become ill? __ Wonder if religious people are supposed to become ill? __ Wonder how God helps people who are ill?

How do you think friends should respond when someone is ill or hurt?

What should Christians expect of God when they are ill?

Bible Study
Mark 2:1-12

Retell this story from the point of view of the different people in each of the four scenes below. The questions can help you. Use them, but don't be limited by them. Use your imagination.

Scene 1 (Verses 1-4)
The Friends

How did you hear about Jesus being in town?
__ Newspaper __ Radio __ Rumor __ One of us had seen Jesus. __ A disciple told us.
__ Everyone knew, because Jesus stirred up controversy wherever he went.

How did you persuade the paralyzed man to "give it a try"? __ We paid him some money. __ We didn't ask; we just took him. __ We took him but didn't tell him why. __ We had been praying together for his healing, and this seemed a natural next step.

When we carried him to where Jesus was preaching, there was a crowd. We thought . . . __ This was a silly idea; why did we ever think of it? __ How will we ever get through that many people? __ They won't let us through because they think that illness is a sign of sin. __ Maybe we should have phoned ahead. __ We've come this far; there's no turning back now.

Tell this scene as one of the friends, including how you got the idea of "dropping in" on Jesus.

Scene 2 (Verses 4-5)
A Disciple Near Jesus

Jesus is standing next to you preaching. A large crowd has gathered. What are you thinking? __ This is too good to last. __ This is amazing; wherever we go, it has been like this. __ This man must be the Messiah. __ I wonder what those scribes over in the corner are thinking. __ This is too large a crowd; something's bound to happen.

You begin to hear noises from the roof, and little bits of dirt and grass from the ceiling begin to fall on you and Jesus. What is your first thought? __ Call the roofing man; we have another leak. __ The roof is caving in; Jesus will be hurt. __ The crowd is putting too much pressure on this small house; it's going to cave in any minute. __ Let's get out of here!

Then a large piece of the roof is lifted off from above, and you see four men leaning over and looking into the room at Jesus. What are you tempted to do first? __ Push Jesus out of the way to safety? __ Call for help? __ Complain at the men for their thoughtless interruption of Jesus' preaching? __ Yell at the men to get down before they make the whole roof cave in?

The men quickly lower a paralyzed friend into the room. It is clear to you now that they want him healed. How do you feel about what they have done? __ Ashamed of yourself for being angry with them? __ Angry with them for interrupting Jesus' teaching in order to seek a healing? __ Filled with compassion and admiring the creativity of the friends? __ Unsure what to do next?

Jesus turns to the paralytic and says, "Son, your sins are forgiven." Tell this story as the disciple, including how you feel about those words being spoken to the man.

Scene 3 (Verses 5-11)
The Scribes

You have been wanting to hear what this new teacher has to say. When some common folk lower a paralyzed man through the roof, what's your first thought? __ These common folk don't know the least thing about courtesy. __ We're the honored people here, and now they'll get in front of us. __ Who do they think Jesus is that they will do something like that? __ They must believe all those rumors they've heard about Jesus healing people. __ Ah ha! Now we can really see what Jesus can do.

Jesus turns to the paralyzed man and tells him that his sins are forgiven. Your deepest belief is that only God can forgive sin. Your reaction to those words is what? __ A sigh of relief? You've always wanted to meet God, and now here he is. __ A gasp of alarm? No man should dare to claim to do what only God has the right to do. __ A "hmmmmm" of curiosity? This is a new twist, and it will be interesting to find out what Jesus means. __ A growl of anger? Who does he think he is?

In spite of what Jesus has said, the paralyzed man is still where he is. You begin to think to yourself: __ Maybe I misunderstood what he said. __ The man came looking for healing. What does forgiveness of sins have to do with it? __ Jesus, after all, is not for real.

Then Jesus looks you right in the eye. He seems to know what you've been thinking. He asks you which is easier to say, "Your sins are forgiven" or "Stand up and take up your mat and walk." Your answer, if he had given you time to make it, would have been: __ I'd say forgiveness; no one could tell if I were right or wrong. __ I'd say "Stand up and take up your mat"; even if it didn't work, it wouldn't get me in trouble with God. __ How dare you put me on the spot!

Now tell this story as the scribe, including the order Jesus gives to the paralytic to take up his mat and go home.

Scene 4 (Verses 9-12)
Someone in the Crowd

It is clear that Jesus is about to have a run-in with the scribes. You know they are very powerful. As the tension mounts, you find yourself thinking: __ Who does Jesus think he is? These are our community's religious leaders. __ Who do they think they are? Just because Jesus isn't a scribe, they want to find fault with him. __ How does Jesus dare say things like that when they are here? Jesus is a good person, but he's gone overboard thinking he can pronounce forgiveness.

Jesus seems to call himself "Son of Man." You know that phrase refers to someone who is supposed to be God's very special person, one who is to bring in the kingdom of God. You begin to wonder: __ Is this the end of the world? __ Has Jesus gone off the deep end? __ I'm afraid *of* him. __ I'm afraid *for* him.

Jesus then turns to the paralyzed man and tells him to take up his mat and walk. In the split second before anything else happens, this thought races through your mind: __ What if it doesn't work? __ If it does work, what does that mean for me? __ What if this is a trick? __ What will the scribes do if the man does walk? __ I'm afraid; I wish I weren't here.

Now tell the story as a member of the crowd, including your reaction when the man in fact got up and walked.

The Disciples ·

A Dose of Realism

All around Jesus were rich and powerful people. Many of them felt threatened by what Jesus taught. Jesus had had some wonderful times with his disciples, but he knew there were difficult days ahead.

Jesus told his disciples what to expect. They needed to know the truth about what lay in store for them. But he also reminded them of God's promises.

Read each of the following Scriptures to see what Jesus expected to happen to his followers and how he encouraged them to remain faithful.

Bible Study

Matthew 10:16-23

Jesus puts warnings and promises side by side. He says he is sending his disciples out like "sheep into the midst of wolves." What does that mean?

He also tells them to "be wise as serpents and innocent as doves." By that he means
__ it's OK to lie but look innocent;
__ wear feathers and speak with a forked tongue;
__ don't be foolish but don't deceive people either.

Verse 17-18 tells about three things Jesus expected his disciples would experience if they followed him. What are they?

In verses 19-20 Jesus tells his disciples how to behave when they get into trouble for preaching. What does he promise them?

Would the promise have eased your fears if you were them? Why or why not?

In verses 21-22 what bad time does Jesus say the disciples may have to endure?

What is Jesus' promise to them?

Verse 23 again describes a problem the disciples may face and a promise Jesus makes. The problem is

The promise is

Matthew 10:26-33

Jesus is telling his disciples not to fear *and* not to keep quiet. He tells them to preach his message out in the light and to shout it from the house-tops. What is there in these verses that tells you that he didn't think it was going to be easy?

Verses 29-31 contain two sayings. They are being spoken to people who were in for a hard time. What do you think they mean?

__ Sparrows are so cheap that you can always buy more if one of yours dies.

__ God is so amazing that counting every one of the hairs on people's heads is no big deal.

__ God knows and cares about even the smallest of things; God will certainly care for you.

In verse 32 Jesus makes a promise to those who are faithful: He will speak on their behalf before God. How do you think the disciples felt about that?

Would that promise be enough to get you to face the same threats as they did? Why or why not?

Mark 8:34–9:1

Again, Jesus tells his disciples about the hard times they will face. Read the passage in the Bible. Then read the paraphrase printed below.

34The disciples were there with a large crowd. Jesus called out loudly, "If you want to be my followers, forget about yourself, accept your responsibilities, do what I do. 35When all you care about is yourself, you don't have a life—you've lost it without even knowing it. But if you try to bring good news to people and show them what it means to be a Christian—even if you get into trouble—you'll know that God and I are there with you. 36What good is it to pile up a lot of stuff if it costs you your closeness to God? 37Isn't your life worth more than a pile of junk, even if it's expensive junk? 38Some day God will complete the kingdom God is starting here; when that happens, do you want to have to say to God that you were ashamed of me? Then I'll be ashamed of you."
9:1Then Jesus shouted to the crowd, "This is the truth: While some of you are still living, you will see that God has come here with power."

If you were in the crowd hearing these words for the first time, what would your reaction be?

If you were a disciple and were committed to following Jesus, what verses would give you encouragement?

Say It Now

Rewrite these Bible verses in today's language. Don't be afraid to be experimental. For example, Matthew 10:27 reads "What you hear whispered, proclaim from the housetops." It could be redone in any of these ways:

➤ If you believe in me, speak out!
➤ Don't keep me a secret—turn up the volume!
➤ Don't hide my message on little scraps in your pocket; put it on a giant billboard!
➤ Don't whisper; broadcast the good news!

Now you try your hand at these:

"See, I am sending you out like sheep into the midst of wolves."

"Let them deny themselves and take up their cross and follow me"

"Do not fear those who kill the body but cannot kill the soul."

"So do not be afraid; you are of more value than many sparrows."

"Everyone therefore who acknowledges me before others, I also will acknowledge before my Father in heaven."

Peter's Confession

Who Do They Think You Are?

Here is a list of several people you know. The question is, how well do they know you? When they think of you, do they capture the real you?

Write a word or phrase that best describes how you think each one thinks of you. For example, when the school principal hears your name, he or she probably thinks "well-behaved." Your kid sister probably thinks "fun—sometimes, at least." Fill in the blanks with your first response.

Your best friend _____

Your worst enemy _____

Your favorite teacher _____

Your least favorite teacher _____

Your nearest neighbor _____

Your pastor _____

Your oldest brother or sister _____

Your youngest brother or sister _____

Your school principal _____

The adults in your church _____

The people you work for _____

Your mother _____

Your father _____

Kids you see only at school _____

Your girlfriend or boyfriend _____

Your coach or band director _____

Your grandparents _____

Your doctor _____

Your youth group leaders _____

Now, go through the list and circle the three that best describe you.

Even the best descriptions leave something out. What would need to be added here to present a truer picture of you?

Finally, what is one way that your own idea about who you are has changed in the last two years? (Something you used to think about yourself that is no longer the case.)

Bible Study
Mark 8:27-33

Mix and Match

Match the following people from this passage to the definitions below. Place the number of the name in the blank by the correct definition.

1. John the Baptist
2. Elijah
3. prophets
4. Peter
5. Christ

6. Son of Man
7. elders
8. chief priests
9. scribes
10. Satan

__ One of the first disciples. His name also means "rock."

__ Not clergy or priests, but still active leaders in the Jewish religion.

__ A fiery preacher who baptized Jesus; some thought he might return from the dead to announce the arrival of the Messiah.

__ A name for a person some Jews expected to bring God's kingdom to earth.

__ Professional teachers of the Jewish law.

__ The name of a being that Jews believed tempted people to sin.

__ An Old Testament prophet whom many thought would return to earth to announce the dawn of God's kingdom.

__ The professional religious leaders of the Jewish Temple.

__ A word that also means "Messiah" and refers to a person who Jews expected to restore Jewish rule to the nation of Israel.

__ People who preached about God and who called the Jews to be faithful and to practice justice.

Getting the Answers Right
Mark 8:27-30

Jesus had been preaching and healing people for quite a while. Now he was heading for Jerusalem on what would turn out to be his last trip. He asked his disciples, "Who do people say that I am?" What do his disciples answer in verse 28?

From that answer (and the definitions from "Mix and Match") do you think that people understood who Jesus was? Why or why not?

Jesus next asks Peter who he thinks Jesus is (verse 29). What is Peter's answer?

Do you think Peter was right? Why or why not?

Jesus tells the disciples not to tell anyone about him. Which of these helps explain what may be the reason why? (You may check more than one.)

_ Peter was wrong.

_ Peter was right, but others wouldn't understand.

_ The leaders would become upset if word got out that people thought Jesus was the Christ.

_ To the Jews, *Christ* meant someone who would defeat their enemies and set up an independent Jewish nation. If the Romans caught wind of that, there would be trouble for everyone.

Getting the Answers Wrong
Mark 8:31-33

In the Jewish belief, the Son of Man was one who would come in power and victory to bring God's kingdom. Jesus had a different idea about what would happen to the Son of Man. What was it?

How did Peter respond?

Judging from Peter's response, do you think he really understood who Jesus was? Why or why not?

Jesus spoke harshly to Peter, calling him Satan and telling him to get away from him. What had Peter done that was so dangerous (verse 33)?

THOUGHT QUESTION

Peter thought that Christ would come with power and should not suffer. Jesus thought that, to be on the side of God, he needed to suffer rather than to take over the nation with power.

Jesus, therefore, called Peter *Satan*. Satan is the one who tempts a person to sin. Do you think Jesus was tempted to become the kind of Christ that Peter expected?

My Creed

A creed is a statement telling what you believe. In fact, *creed* comes from the word *credo* which means "I believe." In the space below, write about your belief in and about Jesus. Put down what you truly believe at this point in your life.

As you know Jesus more and grow in your faith, you may deepen or even change some beliefs you hold now. That's to be expected. At a later time write a new creed for yourself. If you save this page, put today's date on it, and reread it at that time, you will have a way of seeing how you are growing spiritually.

I believe that Jesus is

The Transfiguration

You're So Much Like . . .

Listed below are several people. Most of them probably know you quite well. Who in your family would they be most likely to say you are like? If they already have someone they think you are similar to, write that name down. If not, try to imagine who they might say you are most like.

Your mother? _____

Your father? _____

Your grandmother? _____

Your grandfather? _____

Your sister? _____

Your brother? _____

The aunt you know best? _____

The uncle you know best? _____

Which of them, in your opinion, comes closest to being right?

In what ways?

Choose Your Stuff

Our stuff says something about who we are. If you could choose any three things to have with you at all times to tell others something about yourself, what would they be?

Would you choose a CD player to show that music really matters to you? Would you wear only designer clothes (with the label out and on display) so people would get the message that you're in fashion? Would you wear your cross to let others know you are a follower of Jesus?

MY CHOICE	WHY
1.	
2.	
3.	

 ## Bible Study
Mark 9:2-8

This episode is called "The Transfiguration." The word has two parts: *figuration*, which means to give a shape to something (it referred at first to making something out of clay, the way a potter does); and *trans*, which means across.

Transfiguration means to put a new shape to something right across its old shape. In this story, the transfiguration happens to Jesus—he doesn't exactly change his shape, but his appearance changes in an unusual way.

1. Jesus took with him _____ and _____ and _____.

2. He led them up a high _____ apart, by themselves.

3. When he was transfigured, his _____ became dazzling white.

4. And there appeared to them _____ and _____, who were talking with Jesus.

5. When Peter saw what was happening, what did he offer to do?

6. A cloud overshadowed them, and from the cloud there came a voice, saying:

7. Then what happened?

8. What do these Old Testament passages have in common with the story of the Transfiguration?

Exodus 24:1-2.

Exodus 24:15-18.

Exodus 34:29-30.

9. What do we know about the burial places of Moses and Elijah? They have something in common. Look at 2 Kings 2:11 and Deuteronomy 34:6.

10. Read Malachi 4:4-6 (Malachi is the last book in the Old Testament). What special meaning did Elijah have for Israel?

Christians Transformed

In 2 Corinthians 3:7-18, Paul compares the shining experiences of Moses and Jesus. Moses' face was so bright from being with God he had to wear a veil so people could look at him. Paul claims the glory of Jesus is far greater! The word of hope for us is that, as we set our hearts and minds on Jesus and live in his presence, we are being transformed ourselves into the image of Christ.

THOUGHT QUESTIONS

If you were Mark, what meaning would you hope your readers would get from these parts of your story of Jesus' Transfiguration?

The event took place on a mountain.

Moses was there.

Elijah was there.

Three men accompanied Jesus.

Peter wanted to make three dwellings (booths or tents used in a Jewish festival that celebrated God's act of salvation in the Exodus).

Jesus' appearance was dazzling.

A cloud came over them, and God's voice spoke.

I Am!

Who Is Jesus?

In the Gospel of John, Jesus speaks about who he is. Seven of those speeches include the "I Am" sayings. In each one, Jesus describes himself a little differently, but taken all together, the images give us a greater sense of who Jesus is.

Match the images below to the correct Bible verses. Draw a line connecting the two.

Images	Bible Passages
Bread of Life	John 15:1
Light of the World	John 14:6
Gate (door)	John 11:25
Good Shepherd	John 6:35
Resurrection and Life	John 8:12
Way, Truth, and Life	John 10:14
True Vine	John 10:9

Choose Only Two

Suppose you were the writer of the Gospel of John. Suppose, further, that you didn't have room to include in your Gospel all of the "I Am" statements. In fact, you could use only two of them. Which two would you choose?

Here are some thoughts to help you make your decision: Which images are the most memorable? Which ones seem to say the most? Which one do most people need to hear most often? Which of those images of Jesus speaks best to you?

1.

2.

Tell why you chose those two.

 **Bible Study**

Jesus the Light
John 8:12-20

What does Jesus promise in verse 12 to those who follow him?

The Pharisees criticize Jesus in verse 13. What do they say?

Read verses 14, 17, and 18. Jesus claims that he does have a second witness to who he is. Who is that?

Do you think that, if the Pharisees knew that other one, they would have known who Jesus was? Why or why not?

Jesus told the Pharisees that he was the light of the world. Do you think the Pharisees "saw the light"? Why or why not?

Light at the Feast

The Feast of Tabernacles helped the Jews remember the time they wandered in the wilderness guided through the night by the light of a flaming pillar. The Jews later began to use the image of "light" to describe things that guided them in other ways. For example, the Law, which guided them in their religion, was sometimes called an undying light.

At the ceremonies for the Feast of Tabernacles, on the first night, four large golden candlesticks were lighted. The candlesticks were in bowls set so high that someone had to climb up a ladder to light them. The light given by those huge candles was said to be so bright that it lighted up much of Jerusalem.

Scholars believe that Jesus was standing in the very courtyard where those candles were lit when he described himself as the light of the world. If so, Jesus was describing himself as a light even greater than the light for the Tabernacle Feast. That light illuminated only Jerusalem. Jesus' light was for the whole world.

Why do you think Jesus chose to speak of "light" while standing in that place? Can you understand why the Pharisees were upset with him?

Jesus the Gate
John 10:1-10

Jesus describes, in verses 1 and 2, two kinds of people who have interest in sheep:

According to verses 3 and 4, how does the shepherd relate to his sheep? How does he care for them?

How will the sheep respond to the stranger?

In verses 9 and 10 Jesus describes what waits for those who see that he is the gate. What does he say?

If Jesus calls himself the gate, what would that mean about the other religious leaders who disagreed with him?

Do you think the Pharisees regarded Jesus as the gateway to God? Why or why not?

If the Pharisees were to choose an image for Jesus, what image might they choose?

What would they want that image to tell others about Jesus?

Sheep and the Gate

The gate in this passage is also referred to as a door in some translations. The sheep were kept inside the penned-in area unless the gate-keeper let them out. The gate and gatekeeper protected the sheep from thieves.

During the years leading up to Jesus' time, several men had become high priests and Temple leaders who were, in fact, discovered to be thieves. Those leaders, who were supposed to be the shepherds of the people, were instead stealing from them.

Jesus often referred to his followers as his "little flock." In his arguments with the Pharisees and priests, he tried to protect the people from them. When he did so, he was like the gate that kept the thieves out and let in only those who truly cared for the people.

Read further in John 10 to find out more about Jesus and his "sheep."

Palm Sunday

How Would You Tell?

Rumors are flying like crazy: People think the Messiah has returned! You have been put on a panel of experts to investigate this person. You represent the Christian church and must bring a Christian point of view to the committee.

Twenty centuries have passed since Jesus came. If the person who has come in our time is the Messiah, you believe he would have to be like Jesus.

If you saw this new person, how would you tell whether or not he was the Messiah? What would you expect him to be like?

How would you expect the Messiah to be dressed? (check one)
__ a three-piece suit
__ a long flowing gown
__ like a Jewish shepherd
__ designer jeans

What language would the Messiah speak?
__ Aramaic (the language Jesus spoke)
__ English
__ Spanish
__ all languages

What mode of transportation would he use?
__ donkey
__ limo
__ personal jet
__ he would just appear

How would he speak to world leaders?
__ angrily
__ sympathetically
__ helpfully
__ sadly

What would his attitude be toward each of the following groups of people?

The poor _____

Women _____

The rich _____

Children _____

The sick _____

The homeless _____

The Christian church _____

Other religions _____

Would he be primarily a (check one)
__ preacher
__ teacher
__ homeless person
__ politician
__ celebrity
__ military leader
__ social worker

Which of these would you expect to be among his closest friends? (check as many as you need)

__ revolutionary leaders
__ small town businessmen
__ mayors and senators
__ pastors
__ high school students
__ single people
__ popular musicians
__ movie stars
__ teachers
__ farmers
__ owners of large businesses
__ accountants and workers from the Internal Revenue Service
__ intellectuals
__ famous writers
__ doctors
__ athletes

Which characteristic of Jesus would you most look for as you examine this person?

Why did you select that characteristic?

Bible Study
Old Testament

In Jesus' time, many people had an idea of what the Messiah would be like. Their expectations came in part from the Hebrew Scriptures (the Old Testament).

Zechariah 9:9-10. From this passage what would the Jews expect of the Messiah?

His attitude:

His transportation:

What he would do about war:

How extensive his rule would be:

2 Kings 9:11-13. In this story Elisha had sent a prophet to bring a message to Jehu. Jehu has just received the message from the prophet, has come out from his room, and has been greeted by his servants.

What is the message Jehu has received?

How do his servants respond?

Patriotic Psalms

The Jews longed for the coming of the Messiah, whom they expected would be a great king like David. He would start a revolution, drive out the Romans, and set up a Jewish kingdom, with Jerusalem as its capital. Passover was a festival of freedom, so patriotic feelings were especially high. The Psalms sung for "going up to Jerusalem" were patriotic songs.

Psalm 68:24-25. When the new king came, the Jews expected a parade like the one described here. Where is the procession going?

Who is in the procession?

Psalm 118:25-27. People watching the procession might shout, "Save us!" What's another way of saying that?
__ Maranatha!
__ For heaven's sake!
__ Hosanna!

Verse 26 shouts a blessing on someone. Who?

What is there in verse 27 that might make Christians think of Palm Sunday?

 **Bible Study Mark 11:1-11**

Jesus Approaches Jerusalem

Jesus is preparing to go into Jerusalem. He has already told his friends that he expects to suffer and perhaps die there.

On the way, Jesus gives an assignment to two disciples. What is it?

How do you think it was possible for Jesus to get the colt? (check those you think are true)
__ He had friends in Jerusalem and had arranged for this ahead of time.
__ He had telephoned ahead to the local Rent-A-Colt.
__ Rabbis were able to borrow animals on the condition that they returned them unharmed.
__ It was just a coincidence that it worked out.

Match the Old Testament passages from the first
Bible Study in this session with what happened in
Mark:

Verse 7. _____

Verse 8. _____

Verse 9. _____

Verse 10. _____

All of the events described in verses 7-10 take
place outside of the city. In verse 11 Jesus enters
the city. There is no mention of a crowd, no one
seems to be having a parade or celebration. He
goes to look around almost unnoticed. What do
you suppose has happened?

___ The city was so busy, no one noticed the
parade.

___ Little parades like that happened all the time
during festivals. Most people paid no attention.

___ Jesus got into the city so late at night, everyone had gone home.

___ No one really cared about Jesus, so he turned
around and went back to Bethany.

___ It was basically the poor and the peasants who
really understood Jesus, and they lived outside
the city.

The Last Supper

Certainties

Rate each of the following sentences to show how certain you are that it is true. Circle the number beside each one that best expresses how you really feel—not how you think you should feel. You will not have to show this to others unless you wish to.

1 = I am absolutely certain.

2 = I am reasonably certain.

3 = I am not quite sure.

4 = I find this really hard to believe.

1. God loves me.   1 2 3 4

2. I love God.   1 2 3 4

3. God trusts me.   1 2 3 4

4. I trust God.   1 2 3 4

5. Christ believes in me.   1 2 3 4

6. I believe in Christ.   1 2 3 4

7. Jesus fulfilled his mission on earth.   1 2 3 4

8. I can fulfill my mission on earth.   1 2 3 4

9. Jesus loved others.   1 2 3 4

10. I love others.   1 2 3 4

11. The church cares for me.   1 2 3 4

12. I care for the church.   1 2 3 4

13. The church is good to me.   1 2 3 4

14. I am good to the church.   1 2 3 4

15. Jesus did what is right.   1 2 3 4

16. I will do what is right.   1 2 3 4

17. Jesus kept his faith even when it was dangerous.   1 2 3 4

18. I will keep my faith even when it is dangerous.   1 2 3 4

19. Jesus knew what he believed.   1 2 3 4

20. I know what I believe.   1 2 3 4

21. True disciples never doubt God.   1 2 3 4

22. True disciples never doubt themselves.   1 2 3 4

23. Jesus loves even those who fail him.   1 2 3 4

24. Jesus doesn't expect us to be certain, only faithful.   1 2 3 4

25. God strengthens us to serve Christ better.   1 2 3 4

THOUGHT QUESTIONS

In your opinion, how confident were the disciples in Jesus _____? in their faith in Jesus _____? (Place one of the numbers from the previous page in each of the blanks.)

Tell why you answered the way you did. What examples or stories from the New Testament help explain your answers?

What experiences from your own life help explain your answers?

Bible Study
Matthew 26:17-30

The Scripture verses for today tell about Jesus' last supper with his friends. It is this meal that we remember every time the church celebrates Holy Communion.

Read Matthew 26:17-30 completely through out loud. If you are in a group, assign one person to read the words Jesus speaks, one to read the words spoken by Judas, and one person to be the narrator (to read all of the lines that are not in quotation marks). When there are lines spoken by all of the disciples, everyone should speak them.

Jesus spoke of eating the Passover. What does that mean? (check one)
__ A meal made up mostly of leftover, passed over food.
__ A meal over which no salt has been passed.
__ A sacred meal commemorating the time the spirit of death passed over rather than taking the lives of the Jews in Egypt.
__ A special kind of sandwich.

Jesus instructed his disciples to go into the city and tell a certain man, "My time is near." What could that mean?
__ He did not have a digital watch.
__ It was his turn to have the room.
__ He was nearing the end of his life.
__ It was a secret code, the meaning of which is lost to us now.

In your opinion, how could Jesus have known that someone in Jerusalem would let him and his disciples use his house?

Pretend you are one of the disciples, not Judas, and you heard Jesus say, "Truly I tell you, one of you will betray me." What would your first reaction be?

Judas had betrayed Jesus. When Jesus said that it would be better for his betrayer to never have been born, how do you think Judas felt?

How did the disciples react?

Do you think Judas really believed anything that Jesus said? Why or why not?

Why do you think the disciples all asked, "Surely not I, Lord?"

__ Each wanted to find out what Jesus really knew.

__ Each had begun to betray him secretly to the Romans and was surprised that Jesus knew.

__ They all were genuinely worried that they could not keep the faith during hard times.

__ They were afraid he was ordering one of them to betray him.

When Judas said, "Surely not I, Rabbi?" Jesus answered, "You have said so." What did he mean by that?

__ He overheard Judas tell someone else.

__ He misunderstood and thought that Judas was confessing.

__ He knew that Judas already knew the answer to his own question.

__ Judas had confessed to him earlier.

All of the disciples have just announced their uncertainty—they did not know whether or not they would betray Jesus. In spite of that, Jesus went ahead and shared a meal with them. Why, in your opinion, would anyone do that?

When Jesus took bread, blessed it, and gave it to his disciples, what familiar words did he speak?

Which of these comes closest to the meaning of Jesus' statement about the bread?

__ As we have broken this loaf of bread, so my body will soon be broken.

__ Whenever you eat bread, I want you to remember what it was like when I was with you.

__ God gave bread to feed the children of Israel in the wilderness, now he gives me to feed your spirit at all times.

__ Bread is the source of life; and I am the source of the courage you will need to live after I am gone.

When he pours wine, he calls it "my blood of the covenant." A covenant is an agreement between God and people. What new covenant does Jesus want people to think of when they drink wine?

__ An agreement that God's love will reach out to all people and not only the Jews.

__ An agreement that God will continue to seek out sinners and forgive them.

__ An agreement that the disciples will find the forgiveness they need to carry out God's work.

__ An agreement that God will continue to trust the disciples and their followers in spite of their weakness.

What do you think Jesus is telling his friends to expect?

Passover

This spring festival of freedom commemorates the Exodus of the Hebrews from Egypt. It is called Passover because God said to the Hebrews, "I will pass over you, and no plague shall destroy you when I strike the land of Egypt" (Exodus 12:13b). The plague took the lives of the first-born children in the households of the Egyptians but passed over the first-born of the Hebrews.

Passover is also called the Feast of Unleavened Bread, because the Hebrews, when escaping from Egypt, did not have time to put leaven, or yeast, in their bread to make it rise. Hebrew families usually eat lamb for the Passover meal. It was the blood of the lamb that marked the homes of the Hebrews in Egypt for the angel of death to pass over. When Jesus celebrated Passover with his friends (his Last Supper), he gave the meal a new meaning.

Many people expected that, if God's kingdom were to come, it would come during Passover, and especially on Passover night. The followers of the risen Christ, however, believed that God had begun the Kingdom in Jesus. They continued to share the Passover meal, but used it to remember how God had freed them from sin and death, rather than to celebrate being freed from Egypt.

Christians today continue to share in Passover every time we have Holy Communion. But now we do it to remember Jesus and to give thanks to God for forgiveness and for new strength to be faithful disciples.

The Trial and Crucifixion

Bible Study
Mark 15:1-41

Fateful Threes

Three kinds of people meet with the council to decide what to do with Jesus. What were they?

_____, _____, _____

Three times Pilate uses the phrase "King of the Jews." In what verses does he use the phrase and to whom is he speaking each time?

1. _____   _____

2. _____   _____

3. _____   _____

In verses 6-15, three men are mentioned by name. Who are they and what are they?

1. _____   _____

2. _____   _____

3. _____   _____

Pilate asks the crowd three questions. What are they and how does the crowd answer?

Question 1

Answer

Question 2

Answer

Question 3

Answer

Three more times in verses 16-32 Jesus is called king. What are the verses and what is he called king of in each?

1. _____   _____

2. _____   _____

3. _____   _____

In verse 19, Jesus is in the hands of the soldiers. What three things do they do to him?

1.

2.

3.

How many men were crucified and who were they?

Verse 27 tells us that Jesus was crucified. Once that happened, three different kinds of people mocked him. Who were they and what did they say?

1. _____ _____

2. _____ _____

3. _____ _____

In verse 34, Jesus cries out to God. Three responses are made by people standing by. Which verses do those responses occur in and what do they say?

1. _____ _____

2. _____ _____

3. _____ _____

Three women watched the entire event from afar. Who were they?

_____

_____

_____

The events in Mark start in the morning (verse 1) and end in the evening (verse 42). In between the morning and the evening, Mark has three references to time. What are they and what happens at each?

1. _____ _____

2. _____ _____

3. _____ _____

Did you notice anything unusual about those three numbers? If so, what is it?

The End

SCENE 1
In Pilate's Courtyard

Reader A: Pilate was the Roman governor of Judea from A.D. 26-36. His headquarters were in Caesarea. He was responsible for keeping order in Israel. He used the Roman army to help him keep the nation under control. That army was the mightiest in the world, and the people of Israel had no hope of overcoming it.

Pilate had a reputation for being merciless and cruel. He was very likely to mock his victims to remind them how helpless they were. He was accustomed to have people obey him and to answer questions when he asked them.

Yet, after answering only one of Pilate's questions, Jesus chose to stay silent before him. I wonder why.

Reader B: *(Read Mark 15:1-5)*

SCENE 2
In Front of the Crowd by the Courtyard
(Move to a new location in the room)

Reader C: If it weren't for Jesus, no one today would know of Barabbas. His name is interesting. The first part, *bar,* means son. The second part, *abba,* means father. Jesus called God *Abba*—his Father. Barabbas' name, then, means son of the father. He stood before Jesus not knowing that Jesus was the true Son of the Father who is in heaven.

Pilate placed the two men, Jesus and Barabbas, before the crowd and promised to release whichever one the crowd chose. It didn't take the crowd long to make its decision. After all, Barabbas was a man who had tried to free the Jews. Jesus was just a rabbi—a troublesome one at that, according to the religious powers of the day, stirring up the crowd. The people called for Barabbas.

Jesus didn't protest. He did not wish to see others' blood shed. As he had said at his Last Supper, he would pour out his own blood for the many. Why didn't he say that to Pilate, or to Barabbas? I wonder.

Reader D: *(Read Mark 15:6-15)*

SCENE 3
Inside the Palace
(Move to a new location in the room)

Reader E: The soldiers who took Jesus to prepare him for crucifixion abused him. They also made fun of him, pretending to treat him as if he were a king.

Kings wore robes of expensive fabrics dyed in deep purple. The soldiers put one of their own rough red cloaks on Jesus, as a mockery of an emperor's robe.

The Roman emperor wore a wreath of laurel, a beautiful vine awarded to victors in battle and in athletics. The soldiers placed not laurel, but a wreath of thorns on Jesus.

The Romans greeted their emperor with the shout, "Hail Caesar, Victor and Leader." They sneered at Jesus, saluting him and saying, "Hail, King of the Jews."

They dressed him like a shabby emperor and called him king in order to mock him. Didn't any of them know who he was? I wonder.

Reader F: *(Read Mark 15:16-20)*

SCENE 4
At Golgotha
(Move to a new location in the room)

Reader G: A condemned man was expected to carry the crossbeam of his cross to the place where he was to be crucified. In Jerusalem, the place of crucifixion was Golgotha, which means the place of the skull. The hill itself was nearly skull-shaped. But it was also the place where the skulls of many people had hung in death.

It was customary to give the dying men on the crosses something to ease their pain. They offered Jesus wine, and later vinegar. He did not take either.

Death on a cross was not simple and it was not pretty. The victim's arms were either tied or nailed to the crosspiece. The crosspiece was then attached to a long, vertical post, like the crossbar on the letter *t*. The weight of the body rested on a small stake or bar. Victims often hung for days and died of hunger and thirst. Sometimes, to be merciful, the soldiers would end their lives with spears or by breaking their legs.

Jesus accepted his dying without expressing hatred. They mocked him, but yet he acted with the dignity of a true king. Why didn't the soldiers and passersby notice that? I wonder.

Reader H: *(Read Mark 15:21-32)*

SCENE 5
Close to the Cross
(Move to a new place and stand close together)

Reader I: Many Jews believed that the prophet Elijah would return to aid the people in time of need. Jesus' cry from the cross sounded so much like Elijah's name, that many thought he must be calling out for Elijah to deliver him.

Some Jews had even thought that Jesus might be that old prophet himself. Do you remember what the disciples said when Jesus asked them, "Who do men say that I am?" One answer was Elijah.

Many Jews would also think of another part of the Old Testament. This time, not a person, but a prayer—a psalm. Psalm 22 begins with these words:

My God, my God, why have you forsaken me? Why are you so far from helping me, from the words of my groaning?

Was Jesus thinking of those words? Was he praying that old prayer? If so, was he feeling the deep sadness expressed in the prayer? Or did he also pray the rest of the prayer, the parts that say that God "did not despise . . . the affliction of the afflicted; he did not hide his face from me, but heard when I cried to him" (verse 24)?

Was Jesus calling Elijah? Was he praying the prayer of sadness? Was he praying the prayer of one who knew God had heard when he cried to him. Or did he feel forsaken? I wonder.

Reader J: *(Read Mark 15:33-38)*

Session 23
The New Beginning

Resurrection!

What Would You Do?

It is early Sunday morning. You have been awake most of the night. Your close friend, Jesus of Nazareth, was crucified two days ago.

On that night, just as it was turning dark, a man named Joseph had taken Jesus from the cross and placed him in a tomb. He sealed the tomb with a huge stone to protect it until after the holy day on Saturday.

You have followed everything closely. The other friends of Jesus ran away when he was arrested. You have not seen them since. Only you and two others remain now. It has been difficult since the Crucifixion. No one knows if all Jesus' followers will also be arrested. It feels dangerous to be seen in public.

So you have waited. Waited and worried and grieved. And you've told stories about Jesus to cheer yourself and the others. Mostly, you kept going until the Sabbath passed. Today, the first day of the week, you and your two friends have bought some spices. It is time to properly care for the body.

You head for the burial place talking quietly, hoping someone will be there to help you remove the stone and allow the three of you to enter the tomb.

Read Mark 16:1-8.

Who are you?

_____, _____, _____

What did you see?

Whom did you see?

What did you hear?

What did you do?

Tell why (use your imagination):

94

THOUGHT QUESTIONS

If you were the women, would you tell others what you saw and heard? Why or why not?

Whom would you tell?

Who do you think would believe you?

What would you expect them to do?

If It Happened to You . . .

Suppose that the Resurrection just happened this morning, and you were one of the three people who discovered it. All the others have gone. You and your friends are not considered leaders of the group. But you are the only ones who have heard the word, and you haven't heard it from Jesus, but from a stranger standing by his tomb. So now, in your century and time, how would you answer these questions for yourself?

Would you tell? Why or why not?

Whom would you tell?

Who do you think would believe you?

What would you expect them to do?

Bible Study
Mark 14–15

Mark 14:43-50. This scene takes place in the Garden of Gethsemane on the night Jesus was arrested. Three actions are taken by the disciples, two by individuals and one by the group. They occur in verses 43-45, verse 47, and verse 50. What are they?

1.

2.

3.

If this were all you knew about the disciples, what would your opinion of them be?

Mark 14:66-72. After Jesus was arrested and his friends ran away, Peter hovered nearby for a while. He had promised Jesus that he would never deny him. Right! What happened?

If this were all you knew about Peter, what would your opinion of him be?

Tell briefly who the main characters are in each of these passages and what they do:

Mark 15:39

Mark 15:46-47

Mark 16:1-2

Who's True?

In the closing chapters of his Gospel, Mark has shown the men who followed Jesus denying him. But he shows

➤ an enemy soldier (the centurion) recognizing Jesus on the cross as the Son of God;
➤ a Jewish leader (Joseph of Arimathea) caring for his body;
➤ the women disciples as the only ones who remained close to Jesus through it all. When Jesus rises from the dead, the women are the first to get the message.

If this were all you knew about the story, who would you consider to be the true disciples? Why?

Resurrectable Secrets

The women came to the tomb. They found the tomb empty, but the person at the tomb filled their minds with an exciting new idea: Jesus was risen!

But they were afraid. They had such good news, but they didn't dare to tell anyone. Why? We don't really know.

Now you have some wonderful news too. You have some talents, some ideas, some dreams. But you've kept them to yourself. Why? Who knows? Maybe you have friends who laugh at talents or interests like yours. Maybe you just don't think you're very good and can't compete. Maybe you don't want to put the talent to a test because you don't want to find out how good you are. Or maybe it's just your secret.

What would happen if you found a way to use it—not for you, but for God. What if that talent that has been buried in your heart could be resurrected for God? It's worth a thought. So, without showing anyone or even feeling committed, fill out this sheet.

There are these things I think I can do, but I don't do them much in front of others.

1.

2.

3.

Of those three, I think this one is the best one for serving God and other people.

Two things I could do with my resurrectable talent this week are:

1.

2.

Of those two, the one that would make the best gift for God is:

Therefore, I make this promise to myself. Without telling others what I intend to do or that I have done it, I am going to do this for (name a person) _____ by (name a day this week) _____ .

If I am asked why I am doing it, I shall say that it is my gift for God.

Jesus and
Thomas

What Would You Believe?

People believe a lot of different things. Some seem pretty silly. Members of the Flat Earth Society, for example, believe that our planet is nearly flat, like the top of a Frisbee. If you go too far, they say, you may fall right over the edge.

Other beliefs are quite important. Take, for example, the belief that truth is better than falsehood. No one can put that belief in a test tube and prove it. But what would life be like if we didn't believe it and act according to it? You would never be able to trust anybody.

One difference between silly beliefs and important ones is that we can usually give some pretty good reasons for the good ones. We can usually point to something like the belief's importance in living a good life, or in keeping society healthy, or in caring for others.

You can usually tell a belief is silly when you ask a person why he or she believes it, and the answer you get is, "I just *do,* that's all there is to it," or "I don't know; it's just how I feel."

Mark the statements below that you believe:

___ 1. There are flying saucers.

___ 2. There are angels.

___ 3. There are fish so small they can't even see themselves.

___ 4. In every atom there is a world just like ours, and our world is just an atom of a much larger one.

___ 5. Democracy is better than socialism.

___ 6. Wars are necessary to keep the population down.

___ 7. Peter Pan was a real boy.

___ 8. Money is the best reason for selecting a career.

___ 9. No one has to be poor; everyone can succeed with enough effort.

___ 10. Teens today know more than their parents did when they were teens.

___ 11. We only use ten percent of our mental powers.

___ 12. Spoiled meat will turn into maggots.

___ 13. Sports cars are better than station wagons.

___ 14. "Made in America" means made better.

___ 15. America will never again go to war.

___ 16. Advertising is truthful.

___ 17. Dogs can talk to each other in their own form of language.

___ 18. People who are smart are morally better.

___ 19. Christians are usually nicer people than non-Christians.

___ 20. The most important thing to study in school is science.

___ 21. Pigs are smarter than horses.

___ 22. Lightning bugs are born during thunderstorms.

___ 23. People all over the world are pretty much the same, and they would get along just fine if their leaders didn't interfere.

___ 24. People who take a lot of vitamins stay healthy longer.

___ 25. High school is the most important time of your life.

Now, go through the list again. This time pick out one sentence that you believe quite strongly is true, write its number here _____, and then give some reasons you believe it.

Go through the list one more time, this time selecting one sentence that you think is *really* silly. Write its number here _____, and then give some reasons for not believing it.

Bible Study
John 20:19-29

Scene 1 (Verses 19-23). After Jesus' resurrection, he appears to several of his disciples. Only one feature of the room is mentioned in the story. What is it?

Why do you think John would choose that feature to mention?

Jesus greets them by saying, "Peace be with you." Then he shows them something. What?

Why?

Only after that were the disciples glad to see Jesus. What might they have been feeling when he first appeared?

In verses 22-23 Jesus breathes on the disciples. In the Book of Genesis it says that God's breath breathed life into the first human. What new life and power was Jesus breathing into the first disciples?

Scene 2 (Verses 24-25). Thomas had been absent when Jesus visited the other disciples. His friends give him their good news. What is his reaction?

In your opinion, which of these words best describes Thomas' attitude? (check one)

__ foolish

__ reasonable

__ unfaithful

__ doubtful

__ unreasonable

__ scientific

Did Thomas want more or less evidence than the other disciples had?

If you were Thomas, would you believe the message? Why or why not?

Scene 3 (Verses 26-29). Eight days later, Jesus appears again. Compare verse 26 with verse 19. In what ways are they similar?

What does Jesus' offer to Thomas.

What is Thomas' response this time?

Jesus tells Thomas, "Blessed are those who have not seen and yet have come to believe." How does that apply to Thomas?

Did the other disciples believe Jesus without seeing him?

Doubting "Doubting Thomas"
John 11:7-8, 14-16

Because he did not immediately believe that the disciples had seen Jesus, Thomas has been known as "Doubting Thomas." Do you think he was any more doubting or unbelieving than the other disciples? Why?

John 11:7-8, 14-16 give us another picture of Thomas. If this were all we knew about Thomas, how do you think he would be known today: (check one)

__ Terse Thomas

__ Loyal Thomas

__ Brave Thomas

__ Faithful Thomas

__ Believing Thomas

__ Doubting Thomas

In your opinion, why would a man as brave as Thomas hesitate to believe the disciples' message that they had seen Jesus? (check as many as you agree with)

__ He loved Jesus so much, he didn't want to be fooled.

__ The disciples had been fearful, and he didn't know whether he could trust their report.

__ Like most action-oriented people, he would only believe what he had seen.

__ He knew how dangerous rumors and false beliefs could be.

__ Some of the other disciples (like Peter, James, and John) had claimed to have special visions before (like the Transfiguration) and yet, when the pressure was on, they were cowards. That would make any reasonable man doubt such reports from them.

 **Why Tell That Story?**
John 20:29-31

John's Gospel was written years after Jesus died. Nearly all of the Christians who had known Jesus personally were dead. Keep that in mind as you reread John 20:29-31.

John was writing his Gospel for people who had never seen Jesus. What problem might he have been facing with them?

Why do you think he chose to tell them the story about Thomas?

John tells us (verse 30) that Jesus said and did many things that are not included in the Gospel. He selected stories that would accomplish a certain purpose. What was that purpose?

Do you think he should have added other kinds of things? If not, why? If so, what kinds of things would you have wanted him to include?

The Road to Emmaus

Tell the Story

Have you ever noticed how much easier it is to tell a joke than to write one? Or to tell a friend about your fantastic vacation than to write a theme about it for school? Some stories are just easier to share and to understand when they are told.

Most of the stories about Jesus were told at first, not written. But how can print show us how a storyteller would gesture or smile or pause or turn a phrase just the right way or point?

Print can't do all of those things, but *you* can. You can get a story off that page, away from the eye, and give it back to the voices and the ears the way it originally was. Here are some tips for bringing the story to life:

1. Read the entire story.

2. Find the parts of the story. Most stories have four parts: An introduction, the problem or mystery or situation that has to be resolved by the characters, something that builds tension, and then a solution.

3. Imagine the story. What do the people act like? How would they talk? What would they be feeling? What gestures would they make?

4. Imagine yourself telling the story. Close your eyes and listen for your voice in your own head. Imagine how you would say the words. Try emphasizing different things.

5. Practice it.

Bible Study
The Emmaus Road

Part One: Luke 24:13-21

Follow all of the tips in "Tell the Story" on the left. Your part of the story introduces the scene and begins to set out the problem. Here are some facts to get you started:

1. The two men are walking.
2. It is the Sunday after Jesus was killed, so the memory and grief are still very strong.
3. Jesus catches up with them from behind, and they don't know who he is.
4. The men are surprised that the stranger could have been in Jerusalem without knowing what had happened to Jesus.
5. The disciples still refer to Jesus as a prophet mighty in word and deed. They had not learned that Jesus expected to suffer. They still expected the Messiah to be a military leader.
6. Jesus had been dead for three days, and they had lost hope.

Put yourself in their shoes and tell the story.

Part Two: Luke 24:22-27

Follow all of the tips in "Tell the Story" on page 104. Your part of the story gives some clues toward the solution, but the real outcome is not yet in sight. Here are some observations and questions to stir your imagination:

1. Part One ends with the two friends feeling hopeless and telling their sad story to a stranger (who is really Jesus—but they don't know it).
2. The disciples now begin to tell the stranger about the women having visited the tomb, finding it empty and getting a message from an angel that Jesus was alive. They waited quite a while before telling this to the stranger. Were they embarrassed by something that seemed to be foolish? Was it only gossip, which made their loss worse? Were they simply puzzled by it all? Think about their mood.
3. Jesus speaks to them calling them "foolish men." Think about how he does that. Is he angry? gentle? sympathetic?
4. Jesus begins to teach them. He reminds them that the Messiah was not to be a great military hero, but one who suffered. Think about how he speaks as he teaches—impatiently? quickly? slowly? as though he is passing on a precious secret?
5. Jesus teaches them about himself without revealing who he is. How would a storyteller show that?

Part Three: Luke 24:28-35

This part of the story brings the plot to its conclusion. Something special is revealed. Use the storytelling tips in "Tell the Story" on page 104 and the following ideas to help you tell your part of the story:

1. Jesus has been explaining the Scriptures, telling the men that the Messiah came to suffer, not to bring military victory.
2. They arrive at Emmaus, at the home of one of the men.
3. Jesus intends to go on. How do the men get him to stay and eat with them? How important is his doing so to them?
4. Jesus takes bread, gives thanks, and gives it to the men—exactly as he had done at the Last Supper. Can you make gestures showing the bread being broken, and tell it slowly, as though it were Communion being served?
5. As the bread is being handed out, two things happen almost instantly: The men recognize Jesus, and Jesus vanishes. How would you express that sudden turn of events?
6. Then the disciples each say what they had felt privately when Jesus taught them the Scriptures: "Were not our hearts burning within us . . . while he was opening the Scriptures to us?" Each discovered the other felt the same way. How would they express that surprise?
7. They had great news to give to their friends in Jerusalem. How would they greet them and explain what they had seen?

How Far to Emmaus?

The two men who met Jesus on the Emmaus Road finally knew him because of two things: First, they learned from the Scriptures with him; second, they worshiped with him—that is, Jesus prayed with them and then broke the bread for them as he had at the Last Supper.

As a Christian yourself, you want others also to have the very best chance of knowing Christ and of having the fullness of life that he brings.

Think of walking the Emmaus Road as an image of coming to know Jesus Christ. Not only is it a journey, but it strongly suggests that people come to Christ through studying the Scriptures and participating in worship.

Think of your friends and other people who you want to know Christ and to experience the life he gives. What would you recommend for them? What about for yourself and your own spiritual journey?

1. How often should they participate in opportunities for learning the Scriptures?
2. Where could they do that?
3. How often should they read the Scriptures and for how long?
4. Where in the Bible should they start?
5. How often should they attend worship?
6. How often should they celebrate Holy Communion?
7. Should they have a time of worship (prayer and devotional reading) each day at home? If so, what should they do?
8. What is an acceptable reason for missing worship?

RECOMMENDATIONS
FOR COMING TO KNOW
CHRIST JESUS

The Great Promise

Saying It Out Loud

Some things are easy to talk about. Others you can talk about—but only with the right people. And other things—well, it's just plain hard. How is it with you? What things do you feel comfortable talking about almost anywhere? What things do you find you can talk about, but only with certain people? And what things do you find that you can hardly get yourself to put into words—even when you want to?

Here are some topics. Put an A, C, or S where appropriate in the first blank by each statement.

A = I feel comfortable discussing this ANYWHERE.
C = I can discuss this only with CERTAIN people.
S = I really have to STRUGGLE to talk about this at all.

__ __ 1. politics
__ __ 2. my mother's pet name for me
__ __ 3. my grades at school
__ __ 4. what I got for my last birthday
__ __ 5. Jesus
__ __ 6. what I really think of school
__ __ 7. the most embarrassing thing that ever happened to me
__ __ 8. how much I really know about sex
__ __ 9. who I'd like to take out on a date
__ __ 10. my favorite junk food
__ __ 11. the music I dislike the most
__ __ 12. my prayer life
__ __ 13. my shoe size
__ __ 14. what my friends and I did last summer
__ __ 15. what I want to do after high school
__ __ 16. how I really feel about my class picture
__ __ 17. my religious uncertainties
__ __ 18. my grade average
__ __ 19. drug use among people I know
__ __ 20. what I like on pizza

Go through the list again. This time put a "W" in the second blank by each statement that you WISH you could be more comfortable talking about.

Now go to the list one more time. Write the number of the topic you feel most comfortable with here _____, and the number of the topic you feel most uncomfortable with here _____.

Imagine what it would be like to have the same confidence for the second that you have for the first. In the space below write down four ways you think your life would change if you could be that comfortable with the second. (You will not have to show this to anyone else if you do not wish to.)

1.

2.

3.

4.

Bible Study
Matthew 28:16-20

Matthew packs a lot into a few verses. His last five verses are meant to help us remember many things.

Verse 16. Matthew is careful to point out that there are only eleven disciples. How many disciples are usually mentioned?

Why are there only eleven who go to Galilee?

What do you think Matthew wants to remind his readers of by mentioning that there were only eleven disciples? (Check as many as you agree with.)

__ Judas had betrayed Jesus.

__ All of the disciples had betrayed Jesus.

__ The disciples weren't called because they were perfect, but because Jesus loved them.

__ Even Matthew's readers need to beware of temptation.

The disciples had been sent to the mountains in Galilee to meet Jesus. Mountains play an important part in Matthew's Gospel. What other important events in Matthew take place on mountains? (If you can't remember, here are some clues: Matthew 4:8; 5:1; 17:1.)

What significant Old Testament event took place on a mountain and whom did it involve? (Clue: See Exodus 19:20–20:17.)

Verse 17. When Jesus appeared on the mountain, what two things did the disciples do?

Which of those would you be most likely to do?

Verses 19-20. Jesus commands his disciples to do three things. What do you think they mean?

"Make disciples of all nations"

"Baptizing them"

"Teaching them to obey everything that I have commanded you"

Verse 20. Jesus makes a promise to his disciples. What is it?

What might Matthew have wanted us to remember when he included Jesus' promise to the disciples? To find out, read Matthew 1:23 and see how Matthew described Jesus in the beginning of his Gospel. Then read 18:20 to see what important message Jesus gave his disciples.

Matthew 1:23

Matthew 18:20

THOUGHT QUESTIONS

Remember how the disciples had behaved after the death of Jesus? They ran from him, denied him, and hid. They were surrounded by people who disliked them. If they had been left on their own, what do you think they would have done?

__ told everyone they met about Jesus

__ talked about Jesus only among themselves

__ hardly dared talk about Jesus at all

If they had not gone to Galilee and met Jesus there, how would they have felt eventually about their belief in Jesus?

__ mostly sad and disappointed

__ embarrassed

__ angry

__ proud but uncertain

We know from history and the Bible that the disciples were soon telling everyone, friends and strangers alike, about Jesus. What do you think influenced them most to do that?

__ the fact that Jesus was alive

__ the fact that Jesus told them to

__ the fact that Jesus promised to be with them

Tell why you answered as you did.

What would help you be a better witness to Jesus? Knowing he was resurrected, knowing that he has ordered you to do it, or knowing that he will be with you no matter what happens? Tell why.

Jesus of Nazareth cordially invites you to be his disciple.

R.S.V.P.
Romans 10:8–13